Renew by ph~~~~~~~~ D1346242

0845 0~~~~~~~~

www.bristol.gov.uk~~~~~~~~

B~~~~~~

P'

What You Didn't Miss:
A Book of Literary Parodies

As featured in *Private Eye*

What You Didn't Miss:
A Book Of Literary
Parodies

As featured in Private Eye

What You Didn't Miss: A Book of Literary Parodies

As featured in *Private Eye*

Edited and introduced by D. J. Taylor

With illustrations by Ken Pyne

Constable • London

Constable & Robinson Ltd
55–56 Russell Square
London WC1B 4HP
www.constablerobinson.com

First published in the UK by Constable,
an imprint of Constable & Robinson, 2012

A copy of the British Library Cataloguing in Publication
Data is available from the British Library

ISBN 978-1-78033-688-6 (hardback)
ISBN 978-1-78033-925-2 (ebook)

Printed and bound in the UK

1   3 5 7 9 10 8 6 4 2

MIX
Paper from
responsible sources
FSC
www.fsc.org
FSC® C018072

For Ian Hislop

Many thanks to Sheila Molnar and Sue Roccelli at *Private Eye*, Ken Pyne for his incomparable illustrations, Nick Newman for the cover, Felix Taylor and Rosie Morgan for the photocopying, and James Gurbutt and Charlotte Macdonald at Constable & Robinson.

CONTENTS

INTRODUCTION

All these pieces were first published in *Private Eye* between 1998 and 2012. As well as offering a series of comments on the work of the individual writers involved, they are also a modest contribution to an ongoing debate about what might be called the satirist's tragedy. The satirist's tragedy used to be simply that he (or occasionally she) grew old. Had the *Eye* been founded in 1928 one could assume that the young Evelyn Waugh would have nodded affably over its cradle. Come 1963, alas, when invited by the *Observer* to review *Private Eye on London* – this contained a caricature of the potential reviewer marooned in 'The Old Bores' Club' beneath the caption 'Now that even the Pope is a bloody liberal the time has come for me to die' – Waugh could only acknowledge that 'it exposes me as a hopeless old fogy' and suggest that the book be sent to his son Auberon. Waugh junior, unlike his benighted parent, was 'in touch with modern London'.

Half a century later the satirist's difficulties run a whole lot deeper than this, and never more so than in the specialised satirical redoubt of parody. It is not just that, in an age where wealth, talent and celebrity are seldom backed by self-awareness, certain things – they range from the public utterances of Lord Prescott to Max Clifford's *apologiae pro vita sua* – are, as Craig Brown once put it, 'beyond parody'. At the same time, in an era of cultural fragmentation, a worryingly large number of people wouldn't know a parody if they saw one, or, worse, would fail to see the need for its existence if told that it were there. After all, there must be several million television viewers who imagine that Reality TV is a fascinating sociological experiment, or that Radio One's Chris Moyles is a very interesting young man of whom a great deal more should be heard.

On the other hand, parody – literary parody especially – has always appealed to, and mostly been aimed at, a fairly specialist audience, those capable of seeing the joke or, less pacifically, keen to assert their cultural superiority by carrying the war into the enemy's camp. There is, for example, a memorable scene in Malcolm Bradbury's early novel *Stepping Westward* (1966) in which James Walker, an English novelist with a visiting post at a mid-western American university, decides to walk his class of under-educated students through Swift's 'A Modest Proposal' in which Swift suggests that an obvious solution to famine is for the starving to eat babies.

Nine-tenths of the group are disgusted. It is left to the class anarchist, lemur-eyed in the back row, to wonder whether we shouldn't be 're-evaluating our attitude to cannibalism'. Walker despairs, as one or two creative writing teachers, and quite a few parodists, have despaired before him.

To the problem of cracking parody's cipher, and establishing that a 'joke' is being made – not always as simple as it sounds – can be added a third drawback. This is the difficulty of maintaining a sense of detachment, of not being caught up in the maelstrom one would ideally like to be observing from a safe distance. As Clive James has pointed out, however sharp a scourge of celebrity culture the parodist may be, he is quite likely to become a celebrity himself, with all the dangers to his integrity that this transformation implies. And indeed Mr James once appeared on the *Michael Parkinson Show* reciting one of his amusing poems to David and Victoria Beckham. Even *Vile Bodies*' dissection of the late 1920s Mayfair charivari is occasionally rather compromised by Waugh's dual perspective, in which the author can be found satirising a social scene of which he is himself a part, and sometimes forgetting on which side of the fence he is supposed to sit. Craig Brown, to take one of our great modern practitioners, star reviewer and *Private Eye*'s resident diarist, probably earns more money than many of the people he is sending up: not necessarily a handicap, but something that should always be set against the crucible of starveling resentment in which certain kinds of parody are always assumed to be forged.

None of this answers the fundamental question of what parody 'is' or the function that, even in an age of alleged cultural debasement, it might be expected to fulfil. In his introduction to *The Oxford Book of Parodies* (2010), the late John Gross, while noting that 'it would be a mistake for anyone writing about parodies to become entangled in a search for exact definitions', offers some useful observations on the various forms that parody takes: the thing itself (defined as a gradual heightening of the original's stylistic quirks to the point where it collapses into absurdity), variations such as pastiche (quasi-sympathetic imitation drawing attention to its own facility) and burlesque – again, rarely malign – in which everything is so deviously mocked that the *ur*-text can sometimes be left far behind in the burlesquer's slipstream. A good example might be Thackeray's *Punch's Prize Novelists* from the 1840s, most of which have worn a good deal better than the authors (Disraeli, Mrs Gore, Charles Lever) they were sending up.

All this makes taxonomic sense while not quite managing to explain why Craig Brown, in the guise of Shirley MacLaine, minting one of his nonsense proverbs ('He who wishes to go back must first go away') or, from an earlier epoch, Julian Maclaren-Ross colliding (and colluding) with Nancy Mitford ('His grace doesn't half sound in a wax this morning, ducks') is so horribly funny. The most interesting thing about Brown's last collection, *The Lost Diaries* (2010), is the variety of treatments on offer. There are no procedural givens: different subjects, Brown implies, require different approaches. Some of the choicest extracts are simply near-phonetic representations of pop stars doing their stuff: Rod Stewart performing 'Maggie May' (*'Way kup Maggie ar thing Ar gos umfin ter say chew'*), or Madonna in full, uninhibited flight (*'Ah trahda stayur head, trahda stayon tarp/Trahda playapart, but somehow ahfugart'.*) Here, as elsewhere, there is a faint hint that Stewart, Madonna and their kind are only collateral, semi-innocent victims caught in the wider cultural crossfire. Brown's real target, you infer, is not only the self-absorption of people fatally engrossed in the small but delicious spectacle of themselves, but the lazy, self-celebrating media mulch that nurtures them. Significantly, Madonna's performance is compered by Jonathan Ross ('Like, if I were you, I'd fondaw my bweasts all day, thas what I'd do!') whom Brown pretty clearly regards as a fawning, sex-obsessed buffoon.

In his Oxford introduction Gross considers the claim, occasionally advanced by students of the genre, that most parody is at heart affectionate. There have certainly been parodists who bore no malice – see, for example, Malcolm Bradbury's emollient collection *Who Do You Think You Are?* (1976) – or at least no malice towards a work's creator: Max Beerbohm once produced a devastating send-up of A. C. Benson's sedative prose style in the form of a triolet ('Nevertheless, it is my bounden duty to drone on. And, even were it not, on I should drone', etc.) while remaining on friendly terms with Benson himself. Brown, alternatively, seems positively to detest many of his subjects. This is particularly evident in some of the literary parodies, in which the writer's style is gently, or not so gently, subverted to the point where it becomes a kind of offensive weapon capable of bringing down the imagination that created it in mid-flight. Brown on Martin Amis ('I is a serious') is actually a piece of disguised literary criticism, in which a very slight exaggeration of Amis's procedural tics – the repetitions, the stylisation, the sense that all we are really being asked to admire is the spectacle of the writer writing – realises a final judgement which insists that, whatever the merits of Amis's work, everything in it leads inexorably back to Amis himself. The same note was struck nearly a century ago in 'Song: In Wartime', an anonymous parody of the first wave of Great War poets sometimes attributed to J. C. Squire or Richard Aldington:

At the sound of the drum,
Out of their dens they come, they come,
The little poets we hoped were dumb,
The little poets we thought were dead,
The poets who certainly haven't been read
Since heaven knows when, they come, they come,
At the sound of the drum, of the drum, drum, drum

Here a poem doubles up as an essay on 'What is Wrong with Great War Poetry' and is all the more effective for using mimicry rather than critique.

What you didn't miss – none of whose selections, incidentally, is the work of Craig Brown – may also be read as literary criticism by another name. If there is a theme to its versions of contemporary verse, it is the idea that most of what gets marked down as 'poetry' these days is simply prose chopped up into irregular lines. It is also a reliable guide to some of the contemporary book world's enduring fixations, its fondness for biographies of long-dead Oxford dons or dispatches from 'Planet Amis'. One of its main findings, ominously enough, is that practically anything can be parodied if you set your mind to it. Most writers of any distinction end up exaggerating the qualities that make them distinctive. In the same way, so self-consciously stylised a medium as literature could hardly fail to encourage stylisation. Another of its conclusions, perhaps, is that there is a way in which parody becomes an integral part of the cultural process it sets out to lampoon, the salt that gives the Big Mac its savour. In one of P. G. Wodehouse's Mulliner stories, for example, the fiancée of Egbert Mulliner writes a romantic novel entitled *Parted Ways*, whose success is such that, as Wodehouse puts it, 'Clergymen preached about it, parodists parodied it, stockbrokers stayed away from Cochran's Revue to sit at home and cry over it.'

Parody was a bad idea, F. R. Leavis once declared, as it demeaned the artist. To this one might retort that an excessive respect towards books and the people who write them is nearly always a very bad idea, and also that the parodist is not only there to laugh at the overwrought and the self-obsessed: he is also there to authenticate, and, by implication, to set up a series of spiritual preservation orders on the victims who crawl under his lens. The only thing that keeps certain of the subjects of Squire's *Tricks of the Trade* (1917) precariously alive is the fact that Squire thought they were worth sending up. If, as is regularly suggested, we live in an increasingly relativist age, where people prefer to keep their opinions of other people's behaviour to themselves for fear of causing offence, then the parodist's role grows ever more crucial. It could be argued that Craig Brown is quite as much a moral force as the Archbishop of Canterbury, even if, like the Archbishop, he preaches to an ever-dwindling congregation. He and his fellow-workers are not simply there to express their likes and dislikes. They are also a vital part of an aesthetic process that the modern world seems to have lost sight of: the cultivation of that rare but intoxicating cultural condiment, *taste*.

D. J. TAYLOR

GREAT NOVELISTS
OF OUR TIME

LIFE CLASS

PAT BARKER

They sat in a little estaminet in the market square, a mile or two behind the lines, as the pale Flanders sky sank into twilight. Madame was smoking cigarettes at the till in that indefinably Gallic way French people have.

'Just think,' Elinor said. 'If you were writing a novel about all this ninety years in the future, how would you do it?'

He thought for a moment of the horrors of the day that had passed in the field hospital, Dr Filgrave's hands dripping with pink, intestinal fluid as he bent over an exposed stomach cavity, the severed limbs lying in the sawdust. 'I don't know,' he said, 'I think I'd put in lots of detail. Get the descriptions of Great War medical treatments absolutely accurate. It's the only way.'

'But then,' she suggested – she was a dark girl with short shining hair and full, pouting lips – 'we have a life beyond the war, don't we?'

'Of course we do,' he said. 'After all, we're both art students. You'd have to get that in. I mean, you can't go wrong with art school bohemianism, can you? Plus you could make one or two of those figurative connections that the critics always rave about. Stuff about the artist's technique being a bit like the surgeon's.'

Madame was smoking another Gitane, the ironical creases at the corner of her mouth making her look even more French than ever.

'Oh and of course art students generally get to have more sex than ordinary characters.'

'What about real people?' she said, blushing a scarlet colour that reminded him of the pailful of human guts he'd shovelled from the operating theatre floor earlier that afternoon. 'Should you put them in?'

'Well, who's that artist chap you see at the Café Royal who gets pissed all the time and sleeps with his models? Augustus John. He'd be great in a novel. Not to mention Lady Ottoline.'

'And dialogue?' she wondered.

'Well, some people say you should go for authenticity, you know, have the characters sound as if they really lived at the time you're writing about. Make the reader feel at home, that's what I say. Wow!' he went on, 'that dress is really fab.'

'Do you like it?' she said. 'I got it from Mr Harrod.'

'Yup, you're looking hot,' he confirmed, as an incendiary flew over their heads and landed on the further side of the square. 'Do you fancy a shag?'

'Really, Paul,' she murmured, her soft eyes glowing with anticipation, 'I don't know what you mean.'

PULSE
JULIAN BARNES

THE PHILATELISTS

She'd started coming to the stamp club the week
before Tracey had left him (Tracey had taken the pop-
up toaster, as well as his collection of Jack Higgins
novels, which he wasn't best pleased about). At
first they'd talked about that strip of unperforated
1934 George V penny reds he'd bought almost
by accident from the chap on eBay, and some US
Confederate locals that she was saving up for, but
one thing had led to another, he'd started coming
in to see during her lunch-hour at Milletts in the
high street, and now here they were having tea in
Costa half an hour before the monthly meeting and
looking at a new Stanley Gibbons catalogue he'd
thought she might like to borrow.

'You know,' he said, stirring sugar into his cappuccino, which to be honest he preferred to the
mocha lattes which some of the younger members
went for, 'that 1867 issue with the grille is pretty
impressive.' He didn't want to seem intimidating so
he went on: 'If you like that kind of thing, I mean.'

'Hm,' she said. She was drinking a mango frescato with extra cream, which always seemed to him a tad exotic for the kind of person she was, not to mention costing a whopping £3.20. 'Those Madagascan triangulars aren't bad, either.' There was a pause. 'Not meaning to be funny or anything, Gav, but you really are incredibly tedious.'

'Point taken.' He was wondering whether he ought to get her a proper pair of tweezers from the shop in the mall. 'You're not exactly a sparkling conversationalist yourself, Ange.'

'It's not my fault,' she said. He saw that she'd creased the catalogue cover, but reminded himself that he could always iron it. 'Or yours. That's what comes of being a character in a Julian Barnes short story.'

'Meaning?'

'Well, he's always more interested in the boring stuff that people do rather than the people themselves. Or maybe it's just that giving them all the boring stuff to do makes them boring. You ought to be grateful your hobby isn't rambling, or you'd be spouting paragraphs about the Kinder Downfall circuit and Bowden Bridge car-park.'

'Whereas I just drone on about stamps?'

'That's it *exactly*. It's not that I don't love you, darling; it's just that we've been created by the kind of writer who never lets his characters have lives of their own.' There was a bit of a pause while he wondered whether the rain would let up and she started scrabbling in her hand-bag.

'What's that you're doing, Ange?'

'Come on, Gav! Don't say you don't know. It's the big symbolic moment he sometimes brings in towards the end. In this one I've got a penny black I was going to give you, only the grand climax is that I've lost it somewhere in the lining.'

'Well, I suppose that makes it all nicely ambiguous,' he conceded. He was still thinking about the pop-up toaster. 'Why don't you tell me about that new range of anoraks you were stocking – you know, the ones with the patent zip-fasteners – last time I was in . . . [*continues*].

NOTWITHSTANDING
LOUIS DE BERNIÈRES

Miss Abigail Tweely and Miss Muriel Arch sat in the drawing-room of Honeysuckle Cottage eating digestive biscuits and drinking cups of strong bohea. They were the village of Whimsy-on-the-Water's oldest inhabitants. Indeed it was said that Miss Arch's muslin-flounced wrist had waved from the crowd at King George V's coronation. Outside the whirr of the developers' pneumatic drills could be heard tearing up the previously unspoilt meadow.

'I would have offered you cake, Muriel,' Miss Tweely now said, 'only Mr Bunn the baker has had to close his shop.'

'Poor Mr Bunn,' Miss Arch sighed. 'All to do with the new Waitrose at Nether Gussett, I suppose. Do you know, my dear, I saw a ghost yesterday?'

'Not again! Was it the drowned parlour-maid from Crashing Grange, or the nun who was blown away in a gale – a story, by the way, that I never in the least believed?'

A low droning noise from across the hill now

informed them that work on the new motorway
had recommenced.

'Neither. It was the orphan boy who was killed
in a shower of hail-stones. However picturesque our
lives here, Abigail, it is a great mistake to sentimen-
talise the countryside.'

'Do I not know it, Muriel? Only the other day,
poor Farmer Wazzock was disembowelled by his
own gardening fork. But does it not alarm you, our
being so figurative?'

'I cannot see,' Miss Arch remarked, eyeing the
tractor that was digging up the road outside, and
the copy of the *Daily Telegraph* whose headline read
*Thatcher's Boom: Yuppies buy up old country properties;
rural life changing*, 'that I am in the least figurative.
What I resent' – she paused to shake the paw of her
pet badger, Boffles, who now stole into the room –
'is the determinism.'

'Determinism, Muriel?' A shadow crept across
Miss Tweely's pale, aristocratic face.

'Precisely. The fact, for example, that we all
know you are shortly to die a horrible and suitably
emblematic death . . . Muriel?'

But Miss Tweely had already slipped upon the
letter from Messrs Shark & Vulture offering to buy
Honeysuckle Cottage, fallen full-length into the
fire, and been burnt alive. Miss Arch shook her
head. In her innermost heart she felt like dressing

up as a man and going out to kill some squirrels.
There was nothing like getting closer to nature.

A SON OF WAR

MELVYN BRAGG

Skipping over the open sewer that ran down the middle of the street, palm clenched hotly around the silver threepenny bit he'd found in his aunt Sylvia's Christmas pudding, young Melvyn rounded the corner to the family house. The lit windows of 14 The Hovels, Wigton, shone invitingly at him. 'Ee lad, there's nowt to warm tha like a champion fire to thee grate,' his father had often said. Pausing only to wave to old Silas McTavish, who stood at his gate cheerfully exposing himself to the small children who played in the yard, he darted through the front door. It was grand up here, up north, with these warm-hearted Cumbrian folk, he thought.

In the front room his mother was doing the ironing. From the tearful look on her face he knew that she'd found another dead rat in the overflow pipe while cleaning the outside privy. But northern people got stuck in. That was what they did. They might become peers of the realm or well-loved media personalities, but they got stuck in.

His father sat reading the *News Chronicle*, listening to *Family Favourites*, smoking Players' Weights and doing all the other things that people did in the late 1940s.

Sam looked up. 'Where have you been, our Melvyn?' he asked accusingly.

His mother moved swiftly in to support him. 'Now then, Sam. He's been to his piano lesson with Miss Fotherington-Posh. Like we agreed.'

'You'll be turning him into a lass if you go on like this.' He turned to his son. 'And what's thee been doing to tha hair?'

'Honestly, daddy. It just grows this way.'

'There's nothing wrong with his hair.' Ellen was defiant now. That was what northern people did. They got defiant about their children's hair. It was a wonderful feeling, this defiance. 'Besides, I want him to make something of his life.'

'Make summat of his life? There's a job waiting for him at Carlisle sewage works any time he likes.'

'No. Something *proper*. Like, well, a highly re-spected TV arts presenter, or a best-selling novelist.'

Melvyn could see his father staring at him intently. 'Well, just you promise me one thing, young Melvyn. Wherever you go and whatever you do, always remember where you come from.'

In his mind's eye he could see the white surface

of the ermine stretching out towards him. Soft. Yielding. 'I'll remember, daddy.'

Outside the warm reek of excrement rose into the night sky. Above, the cheery northern stars looked on.

STRANGERS

ANITA BROOKNER

She had always known that it was her destiny to
write novels. For a time the substantial presence of
art had threatened to interpose itself, but ultimately
even this impediment had faded away and the true
summit of her ambition lay unignorably before her:
tantalising, vertiginous, exact. And so the novels
had been written, a shelf of them at least, with a reg-
ularity that to her public denoted merely a mastery
of her material, but which to certain of her critics
hinted only at a uniformity of subject matter. She
was not distressed by these insinuations, for she belonged to a generation that considered intimations
of both praise and blame unworthy of one's notice.

They were very grave and elegant books, stately
in their phraseology, civil in their intimations, well-
nigh Jamesian in their syntactical arrangement,
decorous in their converse and quite devoid of that
insensate relish for physical relations in which the
modern novelist delights. In their form, so in their
content, for they concerned a class of person peren-
nially overlooked by her contemporaries: modest,

genteel people, quiet in their habits, sober in their amusements, timorous even in their vexations. Their subject was loneliness, their theme endurance, their vice similarity.

Occasionally her publisher would venture the mildest of remonstrances.

'Miss Brookner,' he would say (she liked the habitual deference of his address), 'has it never occurred to you to put in a little, let us say, *demotic* into your books, you know, the kind of conversations that people actually have?'

She considered this request carefully. It was to her like the sound of rain falling far off, upon distant thoroughfares, but capable of intruding upon her own vicinity.

'No,' she said finally. 'It has not.'

'I see. And don't you think – forgive me my impertinence, Miss Brookner – that your readers might sometimes like you to address one or two of the issues of the day instead of all this stuff about sad old people in Kensington?'

'No,' she said, somewhat perplexed, 'I do not believe that they do.'

'And there's nothing I can do to convince you not to keep on writing what is effectively the same book but just changing the details a bit?'

'There is nothing,' she said, a trifle sadly, 'nothing at all.'

'Well then,' he said. 'We shall just have to carry on as we are.'

Curiously he found himself consoled by this display of adamantine resolve. Everything was cyclical. Reading this in Proust he had not quite believed it. Now he knew it to be true.

THE CHILDREN'S BOOK
A. S. BYATT

As the train bored on through soft, Kentish night, Elfrida Snitkin devised a story for her children. It was about a little tribe of trolls, fierce and black, perhaps an inch or two high, or sometimes three, who emerged from the wainscoting of the nursery in the silence of the night and wove the discarded strands of tobacco from their father Inverarity Snitkin's pipe into gold yarn. Some of the trolls were invisible, others not. Some were well-intentioned, a few fit only to menace. The gold was taken away and sold to an enterprising dragon, Ancaligon, who resided in the well.

The children listened thoughtfully with pale, stricken faces. Ptolemy, troubled and serious, wondered if the trolls were interested in bi-metallism, of which his father sometimes spoke. Hecuba felt freedom in this beautiful and terrible imagined world. Araminta thought of the trolls' sharp, clever fingers tugging at the hem of her poplin dress. Philip, the boy they had discovered in the basement of the South Kensington museum and brought home with them, sat mute and quiescent in the darkling shade.

'Where be you a-taking me, mum?' he demanded finally.

'Where are we taking you?' Mrs Snitkin, like many English things, and many English novels, appeared at first to be an instance of pure whimsy, but was in fact more complicated. 'Why, it is the happiest chance. Really it is. Why, Philip, we are taking you away to be a character in Mrs Byatt's wonderful new historical panorama.'

He thought of hard, adamantine rock, caverns far underground, white, nacreous jewels in clustered profusion. 'But what do that *mean*, mum?'

'It is the *greatest* opportunity. Why, you will be taken to my house and introduced to a number of persons even more implausibly named than those you have already met: Gentian, for example, and Mauve, and possibly even Floribunda, if she has come back from her eurhythmy class. You will be compelled to watch a great many puppet shows derived from the fascinating books of German fairy tales with which Mrs Byatt has filled her house over the past few years, and learn about the history of early Fabianism which she has been researching in the London Library. You will have to listen to a torrent of immensely stylised conversation of a kind that no human being ever spoke, where quite ordinary words are arbitrarily italicised – *there!* What did I tell you? Like *that* – as in the novels of Iris Murdoch, of which Mrs Byatt is such a devotee. And, of course, you will be acclaimed by the critics. What better future could there be for a slum-lad from Burslem with no seat to his trousers?'

The train was slowing to a halt, amid overhanging woods of beech, and birch and yew. 'Please mum' he begged. 'I wants to get out.'

'That, alas, I cannot allow.' Elfrida's face shone arrestingly through the murk. 'We are in a novel by A. S. Byatt, you see, and there are another 600 pages to go.'

RAGNAROK: THE END OF THE GODS

A. S. BYATT

There was a thin child, who was three years old when the world war began. Her name may well have been Antonia, although this would be telling. But this thin child was not as other children are, being sapient, thoughtful and precocious, eager to walk to school across meadows covered with cowslips, buttercups, daisies, thistles, speedwell, foxgloves [*continues*] and given to reading *The Pilgrim's Progress*, and her mother, seeing this, put into her pale, thin hand a solid volume called *Asgard and the Gods*.

And this book, girt in green with its cover image of Odin's Hunt in wild halloo, was a source of fascination to her, for it told of the world's beginning, and its sacred trees, Yggdrasil, the mighty ash, whose roots ran down beneath the mountain-core, and Llados, with its submerged foliage, deep in the enchanted lake of Llareggub, through which foraged a variety of horn-coated and crepuscular creatures, shrimp and shiny lobster, brittle-star and urchin-ball, all roaming and chewing, silently

ascending and quietly descending, and a multitude
of crabs: porcelain crabs, masked crabs, circular
crabs, angular crabs, Uncle Tom Cobley crab and all.
This Sea-tree stood in a world of other sea-growth,
and the shoals of fish went swarming by: herring
and mackerel, porpoise and porbeagle, dolphin
and hammerhead, tunny on their long journey to
the tin, cod, plaice, rock-salmon and scampi . . .
[*continues for several pages*].

As I have remarked, this thin child in wartime
was not as other children are, and while they were
listening to the radio, playing hide-and-seek or
contemplating their grim and workaday destinies,
she was considering the question of how something
came out of nothing. The mind–body problem
would, of course, come later. In a copy of the Bible,
which a kindly clergyman had also put into her
hand, a nice old grandfather with a white beard
spent six tantalising days making things, ending
this prodigious if somewhat implausible feat with a
warning to the man and woman he had created not
to consume the knowledge of good and evil.

The thin child considered this prohibition faintly
presumptuous, and there was no one in the story
with whom she could sympathise. Except perhaps
the snake, who was agreeably scaly, if not logical,
could not be blamed for the role which its divine
creator had arbitrarily apportioned it – could not

it have been consulted in some way? – and which, if allowed, she would quite liked to have kept in a cage and fed on dead mice. But the vicar was jolly keen on all this, and it would have been impolite not to believe him.

Meanwhile, in Asgard the other gods were getting up to the naughtiest larks. There was great Odin, one-eyed, mail-girt and raven-haired, at the thought of whom the thin girl shivered with terror and excitement, Thor with his pulverising hammer, and Loki – sly, witty, darkly malign yet abundantly enticing – on whom, to be perfectly honest, she had a bit of a crush. The gods in Asgard drank mead, plundered magic rings from the dark smithies of the dwarfs and confronted giants, and the thin child arrived at the suspiciously mature judgment that eternity is likely to be horribly tedious. Anyway, it turned out that immortality was an illusion, for the Wolf Time was upon them, the ash tree withered and died, and everything came to an end. For ever. The black tide of water, rising over the surface of the world, was to the thin child, in another of her suspiciously mature judgments, a form of knowledge.

All this made her want to write.

Back in the real world, the thin girl's father came home from the war, busied himself about the garden and cut down the ash tree whose branches went tippety-tap on her bedroom window and inspired all sorts of fey girlish imaginings, which gives this story a nice circularity. And the thin girl, marshalling her resources, went on to become one of the most eminent lady novelists the world has ever known, eternally beguiled by the idea of myth and determined to bring it into everything she wrote.

But perhaps, looking down from some celestial promontory, her mother wondered whether the putting of *Asgard and the Gods* into her daughter's hand might not have been a dreadful mistake.

Author's note: If my sister Margaret writes about this sort of thing in her next book I shall be furious.

TO HEAVEN BY WATER

JUSTIN CARTWRIGHT

The truth is, David thinks, that being alive is probably better than being dead. The Kalahari bushmen – he has read about this in a book – believe that the human soul is an entombed spirit, that only death sets it free to wander the world at will. Perhaps there is something in this. On the other hand, David thinks, Kalahari bushmen are not compelled to live in central London, with all the fret and fracture that implies. Soon, he imagines, he will go back to Jo'burg. Like the Lorelei it will not stop calling him. Cyril Connolly once said that everyone repeats himself in the end. Maybe South Africa is the repetitive act that distinguishes him. Who knows?

Brian is ordering from the waitress at the bar. She has very thin legs, which are at odds with her plump, décolleté frontage, like a sparrow, permanently tottering forward by virtue of its *embonpoint*. Despite his hearing aid he can hear her trumping Brian's banter, banter, he thinks, being about the only thing

Brian has in his chirpy sixty-something's repertoire. *Yerse, we gossome luvverly pig's fry and bacon 'ere me old china. Can you Adam and Eve it?* Cockneys, he thinks, have the vanity of the artist's model. There is an early evening TV show – he cannot remember its name – in which these jellied grotesques snarl and whinny at each other in their urban patois. Maybe they enjoy colluding in their own patronage. Who can tell?

Brian, meanwhile, is heading back from the bar, the odd, puckering smile on his face signalling his conviction that he has made a hit. Brian, he remembers, was a player – is that the right word? – in import–export back in the Seventies, but most of it has gone. The stroke has left the right-hand side of his face screwed up, like a chevron. But then we are none of us what we were. Seeing him, Brian semaphores wildly, like one of those ancient PT instructors about to embark on a piece of old-fashioned physical jerks.

'David, it is very good of you to have lunch with me here today.'

'Brian, you know I wouldn't miss it for worlds, what with the age we have become.' Brian, he re-members, is a month younger than him. It is his solitary advantage. He thinks of Brian's wife, Evan-geline – those were the kind of names women had back then – and the one time they had sex, out in the jungle, going at it like monkeys on an abandoned tree-root. 'But, Brian, why do we talk to each other in this stilted way, and why do we mention each other's names all the time?'

'David, I think it is because we are characters in a Justin Cartwright novel and our individuality is somehow subsumed into the wider creative framework. How, may I ask, is the family?'

'Frankly I'm worried about Amelia. Artists should perform on paper, not in the sack.'

'I haven't seen mine in a decade. Let me tell you, you are a very lucky man.'

Suddenly the fragrance in the room rushes to fill a space he had always thought empty, and he is out there on the karoo again, pissed out of his head on that Afrikaner termite lager, with the red ants swarming over his feet and Bootie the baboon gibbering in his ear. In the end we are all slightly mad, he thinks. Leaving the restaurant, eight hours later, he finds the ticket is in his wallet. Forty years ago a night with a friendly Soho prostitute cost seven shillings and sixpence.

He walks fast. He wants to get to the airport.

PARROT AND OLIVIER IN AMERICA

PETER CAREY

Olivier: Ah, the revolution, *mon amour*, with its creaking tumbrels and its picturesque effusions of sanguinariness. You may very well imagine the trauma such an inopportune conflagration inflicted upon the poor but indisputably Gallic head of *moi*, Olivier Roquefort Passe-partout Thermidor de la Pont d'Avignon, so delicately accommodated here with papa and mama, the *comte* and *comtesse*, in the Chateau Sal Volatile, where, *ma foi*, though it pains me to say, there was an exceedingly strong possibility that an event of a distressingly untoward nature was about to happen . . .

Parrot: Me and me da was printers, down in the West Country, where we used to swim all nudey in the river like meer-mayds with our bitzes hanging all down a dingle-dangle, with skerricks of light a-snuckering over the grass in the brightsome dawn, and the rabbitses going hip-hoppity-hop . . . [*continues*]. But with me ever in fret lest the excise men should cob us and crib us, or my daddy should die, which of course he did, which is how I took ship for Ameriky.

Olivier: As a child I was thought deaf, but ever could I hear the budgerigar in its cage, and if there was silence between us, still it spoke to me. Thus I determined, veritable *philosophe* that I was, denied so much that was indubitably mine, that I should set sail for a new world of enlightenment, and just dealings, not forgetting – *plume de ma tante!* – Mademoiselle Frou-Frou, to whose hospitable attentions it would have been ungracious, I assure you, not to respond.

Parrot: He was a shy one, that Frenchie. With his bosky talk and his pale white hands, white as the riggly worms in old Mr Stumpy's composting heap at Lostwithiel. Washed up, I was, on the boat's quarter-deck, like a juminy-jellyfish, when he says to me: 'At last I have the choice accomplice with whom I had entreated a capricious fate to furnish me.' 'What's that Monsewer Garlick?' I asked – my heart a-brimming like the sea itself, all gurgling through my ventricles in a briny spurt. 'Why,' he says, 'is it not a fortunate chance? For we are to occupy roles of no inconsiderable importance in Mr Carey's new romance.' 'And what do that mean?' I asked him back, my hands all a shake and my posterior still flat-down on the deck.

'*Vraiment*,' he tells me, with a sweep of his dandy hat. 'It is the most exquisite affair, believe me. We shall travel to America, you understand, undergo the most delightful adventures, meet the most fancifully named travelling companions – Look! There go Lord Hernia and his sister Lady Whitebait – converse in the most whimsical mock-historical dialogue ever committed to the page, savour the most exquisite amatory diversions, and yet – and this, young Parrot, even with my great knowledge of literature, I confess I do not entirely comprehend – receive the thoroughly amiable salutations of the critics, on whom Mr Carey exercises a spell of the most prodigious longevity. Are you with me?'

Well, I had the memory of my da, not to mention sweet Dolly Brisket, with her cooey face and tottersome jubbies, all a bouncing under her pinny, and I was ripe to say him nay, when suddenly shinning down the mizzen-mast I sees my dear Mrs Miggins, not glimpsed since I were a little coney of a lad down Devon way for whom a knocking shop were just as handy as a tree to do my business behind. 'Migsy,' I says, 'is it really you?' 'Why, Master Parrot,' she yells, and pretty soon, a-borrowing Bosun McHearty's cabin for the purpose, I eats her, drinks her and boils her up for breakfast as we say down Devon way, with her a shrieking like a stuck pig under the butcher's cleaver . . . [*continues for hundreds of pages*].

A DAY IN THE LIFE OF A SMILING WOMAN: THE COLLECTED STORIES

MARGARET DRABBLE

A LITTLE LOCAL DIFFICULTY*

'One finds moral problems in the most curious environments, don't you think?' she said. 'That's right,' he agreed. 'Even with the insufficient lavatory paper we're getting here, I can never work out whether it's the manager's fault for not supplying enough, or mine for expecting more. Blame is so difficult to attribute. And then one wonders whether the whole principle of attributing blame is defective in the first place.'

They were sitting in the restaurant of the El-Rippova, Marrakesh's most expensive hotel, to which their colossal joint salaries had well-nigh magnetically brought them, and the lavishness of whose décor awakened in them an agreeable sense of guilt, staring with huge embarrassment at the unordered carafe of wine that had just appeared at their table.

*Originally published in *The Bluestocking's Chapbook* (1965)

'This is very distressing,' he said. 'We didn't ask for this. There is no way of knowing whether it's free without enquiring, which would be a humiliation. If it is free it would be a shame to waste it. But if it isn't free it will be astronomically expensive and I shall resent having to pay for it. And then I resent even more the hesitation, that blanketing of the urge for decisive action, that the situation imposes on me. Why on earth is it so difficult to be a liberal these days, I wonder?'

'It's worse than that,' she said. A fortnight married, they were only just beginning to discover how much they disliked each other. 'You see, it may have been left by that nice friendly waiter you've been over-tipping ever since we got here, and so if we leave it he'll be mortally offended.'

'I agree, that does make it worse,' he said, staring hopelessly at the Biba jump-suit she thought appropriate for *al fresco* Moroccan dining. 'If we leave it, we shall reinforce every Western colonial stereotype to which the poor fellow is prey. Don't you just loathe being English, and rich, and liberal and conscience-ridden and living in the 1960s? I can't blow my nose without thinking of what the conditions must be like in handkerchief factories.'

'Yes, I do,' she said, 'but you must remember that without people like us sensitive lady novelists would have nothing to write about. Look, why don't we simply put the wine on the next table and let another set of guests deal with it.'

'Adroit,' he said, 'but morally evasive, surely?'

'No,' she said, 'just pragmatic.' They went upstairs and had effortful, unsatisfactory sex. Later she would bear him four children, get a job on a TV arts programme, have several affairs and be mildly unhappy, But that was what people did in those days.

THE FORGOTTEN WALTZ
ANNE ENRIGHT

It must have been 2002. I was standing in my sister's garden at Dun Laoghaire, a short walk from the fine house that her husband paid 700,000 euros for from a Wicklow bloodstock breeder, and kitchen tiling that a little man that only spoke the Gaelic had to be flown in from Donegal just to glaze. There I am, just back from Australia and mad – *mad* – for Gordon's gin in its bright emerald bottles, Bushmills, Green Chartreuse, anything. And they are all of them there – my sister, Fiona, who I suppose is the pretty one, her husband Dermot, pulling the ring-pulls off cans of beer with his teeth like the big scream he is, the old ladies up from Roscommon the day and all.

And there was Conor. My love. Who was late. And who I must stop writing about in short sentences. Because it is mannered.

It is here that I see Seumas for the first time, rooting into my bag for smokes, exhaling towards the gravy-coloured Irish sea. My mother was the last smoker in Dublin, but oh such a genteel and elegant one, like Greta Garbo, and I, of course, am her daughter.

Seumas O'Flaherty. Seumas. He is, for a moment, completely himself. Different from anyone else. Not the same. In a moment he will look round and see me, but he does not know this yet.

This is one of the advantages of being the *raisonneur* in a novel. That you know things the other characters are not yet aware of. Irritating for them. But not for you. Like the staccato sentences. I remember every word of our conversation, which is convenient, or this would be a very short book.

'What you have to decide,' he says, 'is what kind of Irish novel you want to be in.'

'Is that so?' I tell him, thinking, as you do, of my childhood in Maynooth, that first lipstick, the Tizer bottles stacking up by the outhouse door, ribbons of early-morning mist.

'Right it is,' he goes on. 'The old comic ones with the engaging patois have gone, you understand. Even Roddy Doyle's turned serious these days. Come home with me, Gina my love, and before you know it you'll be falling hook, line and sinker into a bleakly ironic relationship with an older married man set against the backdrop of the failing Irish economy.'

'Jaysus, Seumas,' I say. 'I'm not sure if I can handle that. What about me mammy?'

'Oh, she dies. Keels over with a heart attack. There's my seriously disturbed daughter to put up with too.'

'Sure, isn't life there to be lived, and all?' I reassure him. 'But how does it end up?'

'It's you that's writing the novel, Gina. I won't say that you'll be disappointed, but I won't say I'll turn out to be the man of your dreams either. Now how about it?'

Just at that moment Fiona comes up and says: 'Did you know that the woman next door has patio heating?'

'I'm not sure,' I say, 'that I can take this constant sub-text about modern Irish materialism.'

'Fair point,' she says. When we were teenagers she went out with Podraig McElligot, who was supposed to the best-looking boy in De Valera Street, and I never forgave her.

Conor is elsewhere. Soon Seumas will look at me again. But not yet. This is called determinism. Like the ghosts of my old life, the short sentences march inexorably on. [*Continues.*]

CHARLOTTE GRAY

SEBASTIAN FAULKS

Cannerley took her to the Ritz.

'I hope you don't think it's too corny,' he said as they stepped into the bar, 'but we *are* characters in a novel about the Second World War, and frankly I don't see why Mary Wesley should have all the fun, do you? Plus, it gives me a chance to be frightfully knowledgeable about the wine list.'

Their table was at the side, and gave a good view across the room, which, like the novel, had an elderly air. Cannerley leaned conspiratorially towards her.

'I don't mind saying that this is a terrifically hush-hush affair. If you decide to join us, you'll be doing a terribly difficult job.'

She resolved not to be intimidated by his public school good looks or the stilted dialogue. 'Why's that?'

'Well, the publishers are looking for big sales, which means you'll have to sleep with an RAF pilot and put up with lots of sentences like "When she heard him gasp, 'No', she knew that it was the last thing he meant as the flesh inside her fingers

swelled and seized." Then again, the author's a bit of highbrow, so you're going to have to mug up on Proust and that kind of thing. I won't beat about the bush; we've got to get the *Daily Mail* and the *London Review of Books* on our side.'

'I think I can stand it. Anything else I ought to know?'

''Fraid so, my dear. You're going to have to wear a minutely itemised period wardrobe so that the author can show off his research.'

Outside the mist stole down from Piccadilly in one of those haunting descriptive passages so important to break up the dialogue.

'And it will give you the chance to put your French to good use. There's always a need for fluent French speakers in English novels these days, so they can bang on about Paris and so forth and make everybody feel culturally superior.' He paused. 'Well, will you do it?'

Charlotte's lip quivered, like the loganberry mousse that had just been set before her. 'What if it all goes wrong? What if our cover's blown?'

'No chance of that. All the reviewers have been sworn to secrecy.'

She nodded. Together they walked out of the restaurant, through the dark, carless streets and into the *Sunday Times* bestseller list.

PAST IMPERFECT

JULIAN FELLOWES

I had not seen my old friend – and of late embittered enemy – Peregrine Barrington-Smythe for nearly thirty-five years. Consequently it was with a certain amount of perturbation, not to say puzzlement at what the French call *une situation vraiment péculierè*, that I embarked upon the journey to what the more vulgar of our newspapers would probably refer to as his 'country pile'.

As I negotiated my automobile along the cramped Surrey lanes, now alas made hideous by the mock-Tudor habitations of parvenu stockbrokers, I considered the problem of Peregrine ('Perry' to his *intimes* although, as we knew to our cost, the intimacy was his to grant, not ours wantonly to solicit) whom, to a certain degree, I may be said to have invented.

Although never 'one of us' in the accepted sense (Lloyd's money, then as now, bearing the unavoidable taint of commerce), not even nay-saying quidnuncs could deny that he was an unmitigated success, that his fortune was titanic, his lustre undimmed, his *éclat* unsilenced – the latter quite immoderately so. Yet his house, I must confess, alarmed me. While not traditional in an aristocratic sense, its authenticity may be said to have remained resolutely unproven. Clipped, terraced gardens, gleaming caryatids, Lutyens-style façade, regiment of maid-servants – all these gestured at a desire for only partly concealed ostentation that . . . [*continues for several pages*].

Admitted to the residence by a grovelling butler, I came upon him in his study – a faintly unreal sanctum, picturesquely furnished and revealing a spirit I had not previously associated with him – tottering by an altogether splendid piece of furniture which the uninformed would doubtless term a day-bed but I knew by its correct designation of *duchesse brisée*. He did not look well.

'So there you are,' he said as I advanced, stubbing my toe against a particularly fine Louis XVI commode, not dissimilar to one I had once had the pleasure of relieving myself in while dining at Apsley House. 'And about bloody time, too.' I saw, with an instinctive feeling of trepidation, not experienced since that day at Magdalene when the Hon. Jasper de Toffe alleged that he could not find my name on the Winchester Old Boys' list, that Perry was Perry still. 'I need to speak to you. You see, I'm dying.'

'My dear chap,' I said, as we proceeded to the dining-room, an oddly muted affair of William Morris-cum-Matalan *dishabillé*. 'What on earth of?'

'Terminal snobbery, I'm afraid. Picked up at Queen Charlotte's ball in 1969. The medics say there's nothing they can do . . . [*continues endlessly*].

BRIDGET JONES:
THE EDGE OF REASON
HELEN FIELDING

Friday 3 December

9st 3, bank balance £2 million, no. of phone calls from publisher asking 'where is it?' 17

7 a.m. Am never going to write Bridget Jones nonsense again. Feel have moved on into new phase of career. Will be significant woman novelist in manner of M. Drabble, or F. Weldon. Plus integrity v. important.

8.30 a.m. But then is v. nice getting profiled in *Vogue*, *Tatler*, *E. Standard* etc. Also feel have duty to us Singletons who need advice on important things. Plus publisher is saying they have given v. big sum of money and where the bloody hell is it. Perhaps will write one more B. Jones and then become mysterious literary recluse. Or something.

10 a.m. Problem is what to put in book.

10.15 a.m. Ooh. Could mention friends like Colin Firth, Nick Hornby, Salman Rushdie who will then be v. pleased and give quotes for jacket.

10.30 a.m. Other problem is what to put in after that.

11.45 a.m. Am marvellous, am fantastic. Filled with new vigour and positive thought. Have decided to recycle old newspaper columns in *Independent* and *Daily Telegraph*. Brill. Is v. easy being successful writer, have decided. Off go. Wheee! Print out book and send to publishers.

3 p.m. Aargh. Dozens of reviews in *Guardian*, *Observer* etc. saying book is dismal, unfunny stereotyping of Singleton women, is this what feminism fought for etc.

Later . . .

9st 0, good reviews 0, sales of book 200,000.

Hah! You see what one can do when one is empowered new person? Feel v. sorry for bitter, twisted critics who clearly cannot write books themselves. Think will just have little glass of wine and cigarette . . . [*continues indefinitely*].

THE NORTHERN CLEMENCY

PHILIP HENSHER

It was 1974 in Sheffield and the Fothergills were having a party. The guests ate Coronation Chicken, hula hoops, Black Forest Gateau, potatoes wrapped in foil with cocktail sticks spiked with cheese and pineapple, Jaffa cakes, pots of Ski yoghurt and . . . [*continues for several pages*].

'Hello, how do you do?' Graham Fothergill, dressed in a blue suit with moderately flared trousers and wearing a pair of those platform shoes that were so fashionable at the time, remarked to the neighbour standing nearest to him. 'I work in insurance.' 'Do you?' the man wondered. 'That's terribly interesting. I'm at the Gas Board. I was just admiring your wallpaper.' 'Were you?' Graham said. 'That's very kind of you. We quite like it too.'

Ten feet away Evadne Fothergill was talking to Mrs D'Ulle, her friend from two doors down. 'What a nice party,' Mrs D'Ulle said, 'really festive.' 'I'm glad so many people have come,' Mrs Fothergill told her, 'it being the middle of August.' 'Yes, a good

many people do go on holiday then, don't they?'
Mrs D'Ulle observed. 'We're going to Jersey.' 'Are
you? How interesting. We're going to Dorset. Isn't
the price of everything terrible these days?' 'Yes isn't
it? Do you think Mr Heath will win the election or
Mr Wilson?'

Fourteen-year-old Millicent Fothergill, lurking by
the sofa, thought to herself: I hate them all. I'd much
sooner be upstairs reading *Jackie* magazine, trying
on my starter bra and listening to my Osmonds
records. One day I'll write a novel and put them all
in it and get my own back, and then they'll all be
sorry, eh up, reet mardy crowd that they are [*other
picturesque examples of local idiom follow*].

'. . . Yes, there are new people moving in at
Number 21,' she heard Mrs Crasher saying. 'The
Teigh-Deheighams, I think they're called. At least,
that's what my friend Mrs Crackanthorpe said when
we were last walking our King Charleses together.'
'Do have some more wine,' Graham told her,

proffering the bottle of Mateus Rosé in its wheaty cradle. 'There's red or white.' 'Red *or* white,' Mrs Crasher remarked. 'I can see you're coming up in the world. Just the kind of man who'll be shopping at the new Sainsbury's when it opens.'

'Is it time for the miners' strike yet?' the man who had admired the wallpaper asked. 'No,' Graham told him sadly. 'I'm afraid that's not due for another two hundred pages . . .' [*continues endlessly* . . .].

KING OF THE BADGERS

PHILIP HENSHER

In recent years the little North Devon town of Ditchwater had been left, if not to its own desires, then certainly to its own devices. Successive waves of incomers – tourists, the benignly retired, the reclusively artistic – had come, looked, stayed, gone or inconclusively hovered. Its high street, built in the first flush of Victorian municipal certainty, but now less commercially adroit, had been colonised by artefact-sellers, by a good but not excellent patisserie, a vendor of Sri Lankan batik work, its stock replenished by twice-yearly jaunts to Trincomalee, by choice herbal emporia . . . [*continues for several pages*]. But now there had come to its placid and largely unprofaned streets a writer, who taught part-time at the local university, and here had he set a novel, which began with the abduction of a neglected proletarian child from the altogether ghastly council estate on the town's less civilised margin.

* * *

Like the surface of a stagnant pool driven into unthought-of patterns by the rain, like moor-hens chivvied out of dense undergrowth by a questing fox, like an ant-horde prised from beneath its hill by inopportunely administered hot water, the guests began to arrive at Cyril and Evangeline Deadleigh-Dulles' house-warming party. 'How very nice to see you,' Evangeline found herself saying to a polite woman named Mrs Snoring, 'and have you lived here long?' 'I think we've been here six years,' said Mrs Snoring with the ruminative imprecision she brought to all Ditchwater conversations. 'Or possibly seven. I say, these fairy-cakes are not to be trifled with, are they?' 'No indeed,' Cyril countered. 'Almost as good as the ones we used to buy in Budleigh Salterton. But really, isn't it dreadful about the little girl going missing?' 'Terrible,' said Silas Baugh, who had just come in to the room and stood wiping his feet with impressive rectitude on the mat. 'Absolutely terrible. But do you know they have some new P. D. Jameses in the second-hand shop? Tell me, who is the young man with the lipstick and the Bermuda shorts. Is he a friend of yours?' 'Oh I think he's strayed in from another party,' Evangeline found herself saying. 'These social juxtapositions are so amusing, aren't they?' 'Yes they are,' Mrs Snoring tremulously interjected. 'But where on earth did you buy your antimacassars?'

* * *

Two doors down at Bijou Cottage, Butch and Esmé were preparing for the descent of a tribe of their gentleman friends. Though they imagined that their drawing-room was no more outrageously cluttered than anyone else's, they had, of course, cleared away one or two things: the Ming vases acquired by Esmé's great-great-great uncle in the sack of Peking, Frith's 'Visit to the Fruit Market at Rouen, September 1869', a number of examples of particularly good Breton ware bought on an autumnal excursion to Quimper . . . [*continues*]. Condoms, dildos and jars of Vaseline lay in the Hagi tea-bowls in which Butch usually displayed a rather enticing pot-pourri of his own devising. 'Do you suppose,' Butch now remarked, 'that Tinky and Winky will bring that amusing friend of theirs with the enormous todger?' 'Well if they do,' Esmé said, turning over an Ezra Pound first edition with a delicately poised finger-tip, 'I jolly well want first go of him. You can wait your turn like any other ageing old uncircumcised queen.' 'Oh, *Es*,' Butch said. 'Shall we listen to some Rimsky? And isn't it a shame about that little girl?' 'Yes it is, isn't it. Do you think they'll want these *roulades* for dessert, or what about that marvellous cheese that Quentin brought back from St Jean de Pied Port?'

* * *

'Terribly exhausting, isn't it, the gay life?' Esmé remarked eight hours later, as the last of their guests had debouched into the pallid, unremarkable dawn and the scent of poppers rose on the fetid, smoke-crazed air. 'So much worse, of course, when you don't know what kind of novel you're in. I mean, is this a study of provincial English life built on a unifying transgressive event? Or just the modern gay lifestyle all over again?' 'I say, Es,' Butch remarked, the cocaine dribbling out of his nostrils like vagrant cotton wool, 'let's give all this up, shall we, and get married? No more orgies at the Bat Cave or chatting up waiters, just good old monogamy.' 'Yes, let's,' Esmé said. 'And there's a nice leg of lamb in the fridge, too.'

* * *

They found the little girl somewhere in the end. But she doesn't have much to do with this story.

THE STRANGER'S CHILD

ALAN HOLLINGHURST

After dinner they sat in the drawing-room, beneath a haze of fine writing. It was the summer of 1913, and all the integuments of their particular literary tomb were in place: the references to Lytton Strachey's *Landmarks in French Literature*; the snatches from popular songs of the day; the hints of impending conflict. Nothing in the way of establishing detail had been omitted.

Leaning over discreetly to observe George's nice young aristocratic friend, the lordly toss and thrust of whose pole her brother had so admired when he first saw him punting on the Cam, she saw, to her immense satisfaction, that Cecil was staring back at her.

'I say, Daffers old girl,' he murmured. 'These jolly old social gatherings give me the blinking pip. But I've written you a bally verse or two. See what you think.'

With trembling hands, she arranged the scrap of paper on her lap.

> The book left out beneath the trees
> Is whipt by an ancestral breeze
> Here wends another minstrel strummer
> To hymn that prelapsarian summer
> Stands the church clock at ten to four?
> Yea, we have passed this way before.
> More eager hands to work the bellows
> Of a fire last lit by Julian Fellowes . . .

'Oh, Cecil,' she whispered moistly, 'it's too, too divine.'

* * *

Upstairs in the guest bedroom, parlour-maid and pantry-boy exchanged glances over the stained and reeking sheets.

'What them two young gentlemen have been up to, I hardly care to think,' Veronica declared. 'Nocturnal missions ain't the half of it.'

'That Mr Cecil pinched my cheek and told me I were a lovely lad,' Jonah admitted.

'Nay, that malarkey ain't for the likes of us,'

Veronica chided him. 'Comic relief. That's what we're here for. That and the unobtrusive illustration of the social inequalities of a bygone age.'

* * *

As Cecil dived deep into the hidden pool, lost and secret amid the dappled woods, George watched the polished alabaster of his torso merge into the water's green occlusion. Then, as his friend rose, all naked and marmoreal, to the bank, he said:

'Isn't this the moment for me to take you back to the house, get out my, er, *membrum virile* and shag you senseless over the back of a Louis XVI *escritoire*?'

'Actually, no. Apparently we're going for the Downton Abbey market this time, so discreet fumbling in the hammock is all you're allowed.'

'But Cess, Mr Hollinghurst is *famous* for his depictions of uninhibited gay sex.'

'I know, but he's fifty-seven now, and one has to calm down sometime. Besides, I think he wants the critics to acclaim his fully fledged maturity.'

'Not even surreptitious oral congress in a private box at *L'après-midi d'un faune*? I've got a handkerchief.'

'No! Look ducky, you're becoming as overwrought as Mr Hollinghurst's style. Never mind, we can still have impossibly artificial conversations about art and literature. That's before I die, of course, and get turned into Rupert Brooke, while Daphne marries my brother.' The water dripped like melted butter from his snow-white thighs, his arms sunburnt and sinewy, calves darkly hairy . . . [*continues*]. 'Now, shall we go and listen to *Traviata*?'

'Oh, Cess . . . *let's*!'

ABOUT A BOY

NICK HORNBY

Will Goodbloke sat in the cafe on Upper Street – they'd just come back from a browse in Retro-Vinyl and he was still upset about missing that La's album – drinking cappuccino out of a styrofoam cup. He wondered about styrofoam. Was it a sort of plastic that they boiled up in vats, or just a kind of waterproof cardboard? It was funny there was never anything about it on TV, he thought. Angie looked up from telling him about her ex's psoriasis and said:

'You're very quiet.'

'Yeah.'

'Any special reason?'

Right. Will knew she wanted to talk to him in that way women sometimes did, while you wanted to watch a crap Steve Martin film or eat barley sugars.

'Umm . . . It's just that I never get any proper dialogue.'

'You don't?'

'Well, we're in a Nick Hornby novel aren't we? It's

just' – he knitted his brows together thoughtfully so she could see he really meant it – 'your everyday banalities. I mean, the things people say, you know.'

She smiled at him in that smiley way. 'That's right. But redeemed by the sincerity of the way we say them, I suppose.'

'Yeah.'

'It's like our, well, thought processes too. The way we just, you know, think the mundane things people think, about oh, I don't know, guys and sex. And sex and guys. Oh and kids of course.'

God, Will thought. He'd seen that coming. The conversations at the Sad Thirtysomething Bachelors Support Group in Tufnell Park had certainly sharpened him up.

'Do you mind?' she asked. "About the kids, I mean?'

'No,' he said, thinking regretfully about that La's album and wondering if you could get it by mail-order. 'Fucking A really. Do you mind if I cry a bit though?'

'I've got a handkerchief somewhere.'

He knew then, beyond any shadow of a doubt, that the reviews were going to be OK.

SOMETHING TO TELL YOU

HANIF KUREISHI

Oh *maan*, did I ever tell you about the Seventies? Well, there was this chick called Ajita and we used to go over to her auntie's place in Hounslow and take off all our clothes and lie in the back garden and I'd run my moist, jungly tongue along her sweating . . . [*continues for several pages*]. Only then she went away and it ruined my life. Really, it did. But anyway, about the Seventies. I mean, politics was really right-on in the Seventies. I was living in this squat in Hammersmith, Shepherd's Bush, somewhere, with these Maoists and Trotskyists and radical types and sometimes we'd go on protest marches and jeer at the pigs, though of course this didn't get in the way of all those crazy times I spent with Ajita round at her dad's house, with the smell of the Vesta beef curries rising from the kitchen, and the way she'd lie there in her auntie's garden and sweetly bid me to explore . . . [*continues for several more pages*].

Didn't Nietzsche or someone say that 'sexual passion is the most perfect manifestation of the will to live'? I mean, how cool is that? Of course, all this time I was worrying about my career, I mean whether I should be a writer or a theatre director or a rock singer, or simply hang out with women . . . And then of course there was the music. I mean, music was great in the Seventies. There were punks and Goths and hippy flotsam. Maybe there weren't Goths yet, I can't remember, but anyway the music was great. In fact it was almost as good as the drugs which Valentin and the Wolfman and all those brave, estimable people I knew used to score for me in the King's Road after we'd been shop lifting and pissing on the pavement and doing all those things that crazy young cats used to do in the Seventies. Not that the capacity for happiness hadn't left me, you understand, for my life was essentially an exhausted, ground-down, sempiternal twilight. Oh yes it was.

And now I'm a psychoanalyst, which is still pretty cool, don't you think, what with all the sexy stuff my clients tell me, and my friend Henry the director and my mad sister Miriam in her crazy house up West. And Rafi my son, well he keeps me in touch with what young people are thinking and saying, yo bruv sho enuff he do. Which makes me wonder, when he gets to sex, how will he want it? Will he want to be spanked while being fellated by a negro transvestite? I did a murder once, you know, no really I did.

Publisher's Note: Messrs Faber would like to apologise for the fact that, while advertised as a novel, *Something to Tell You* is, like everything else Mr Kureishi has written merely a projection of his own life, opinions and sexual obsessions. But what can you do?

SOLAR

IAN MCEWAN

He belonged to that class of novelist – vaguely unprepossessing, earnest, left-liberal, often sexually obsessed – who were unaccountably attractive to the editor of the *Guardian Saturday Review* and the judges of literary prizes. But the Ian McEwan of this time was a man of deeply depressed sensibilities, chthonic, limitrophic, and prone to use words whose meanings many of his readers would find themselves forced to look up in dictionaries. He did not know how to write a novel that did not depend for its effects on vast amounts of background research, or wholly implausible moments of lurid drama, and the discovery produced in himself, among an array of contending emotions, intense moments of shame and longing.

Apparently there was a certain kind of novelist – in furtive, emulative moments he had read about them in the pages of high-brow literary reviews – who was able to write convincing panoramas of the world which he and his fellow-citizens might be thought to inhabit: authentic, untrammelled, indisputably his own man (he had been a feminist once, and the phrase still filled him with disquiet). But he himself was reduced to writing immensely stagy productions set on the day of the anti-Iraq war protest march, in which brain surgeons exchanged dialogue filched out of medical textbooks, or laboured accounts of the sexual incompatibility of honeymooning couples on the south coast.

What did Ian do to quench this unyielding desire to be *echt*, to be original, to write the kind of book that would not have the knowing young critics roll their eyes with boredom? Did he write a novel about one or two ordinary people living more or less believable lives far beyond the glare of the media or the international body politic? No, he decided to write a novel about climate change featuring a much-married Nobel Prize winner whose best days are behind him. He knew, as he set about the task, that he should not have done it. At the same time the lure was irresistible. Waterstone's, he believed, would make it their book of the month. He would be able to reuse all the material brought back from the trip to the Arctic Circle in 2005, and with luck no one would remember that an account of this voyage had already appeared in the *Guardian*. He would employ that puzzling, ineluctable garnish so tantalisingly absent from his work – *humour*. And he would be able to read a great many books – already the prospect brought a bulge to his gleaming, Gollum-like eyes – about Einstein and string theory.

But there was one thing, he told himself, as the novel took shape beneath his fond yet exacting gaze, as he despatched countless emails to members of the scientific community at the Potsdam Institute for Climate Impact Research and the Centre for Quantum Computation at the University of Cambridge, and tried to think of some jokes – jokes, alas, were really not his thing. He would not put in one of those jaw-dropping coincidental tragedies that upstart reviewers were sometimes prone to mock. But then, unaccountably, unforeseeably, as his hero walked into the room where the research assistant who had been sleeping with his wife sat on the sofa, an unconquerable urge took hold of him and, with a swift, unregretful stroke of the pen, he had the man lose his footing on the carpet and smash open his skull on the table-edge. When Ian had committed this act he sat for a moment before the laptop, broken, disillusioned, almost weeping at his lack of self-control.

But it was no good. There it was. *'No breathing. No pulse. There was a halo of blood under his head about nine inches across, and for some reason it did not grow larger.'* Then he gave a sigh of relief. A writer must be true to his inner nature. It was all he could do. Emboldened he picked up the copy of *Quantum*

Physics for Beginners and began once more to rifle through its dog-eared pages. Outside the sun slid like a bloody disk over the weary horizon of the ground-down earth . . . [*continues*].

BEATRICE AND VIRGIL

YANN MARTEL

THE SAD STORY OF YANN

There was once a man named Yann. Several years ago, Yann wrote a novel called *Life of Pi*. And when the people read it they said 'Hurrah for Yann!', and a nice person at the *Guardian* said it was 'suffused with wonder', and the judges of the Booker Prize exclaimed, 'We agree! Long live Yann!', and Yann went back to Canada with an enormous suitcase full of money and was very happy. But of course, if one writes one book and the book is good it is then necessary to write a second one, and so Yann, who was a very meticulous and thorough person, sat in his room for weeks and months on end and wrote another novel.

But whereas the first one had been about some animals on a boat, this one was very serious and grim and all about the Holocaust. And when the nice people in England who had published the first book read it they looked at each other with worried faces, and gave Yann a plane ticket to fly all the way across the big, blue Atlantic Ocean, and when he arrived in London they took him to an expensive restaurant, where, politely but firmly, they explained to him that, alas, the book was not very good and all the people, instead of saying 'Hurrah for Yann!', would say 'Boo to Yann!' and other things even less complimentary.

And when Yann heard these words he was very cross, and he stamped his foot on the ground in his rage and went back to Canada, where he took to playing the clarinet and working incognito in a restaurant, although, being a very meticulous and thorough person, he continued to answer his fan-letters. And then one day, when these occupations had started to fail him, he began to write a story about a successful novelist called Henry (not Yann, obviously!) who writes a book about the Holocaust. And when his publishers read it they look at each other with worried faces, and they give Yann – I mean Henry – a plane ticket to fly all the way across the big, blue Atlantic Ocean, and . . . Anyway, one day Henry gets a letter from a fan who is writing a play about two characters called Beatrice and Virgil. When Henry goes to visit the fan, who is a taxidermist, he discovers that Beatrice is a donkey and Virgil is a monkey, and the terrible things that happen to them might just be an allegory for the Holocaust. As you can imagine, Henry *is very excited* about this.

And Yann, being a very meticulous and thorough

person, tried very hard to give this story about Henry and the taxidermist and Beatrice and Virgil some pizzazz. He included a fascinating section about the art of taxidermy, and some very interesting information about the howler monkey, whose roar exceeds that of the cry of a peafowl, a jaguar, a lion, a gorilla *and* an elephant. He put in some truly arresting sentences ('Words are cold, muddy toads trying to understand sprites dancing in a field – but they're all we have, I will try') and a great many references to Flaubert, Diderot, Beckett and Apuleius and other classic authors.

And then there came a day when Yann's publishers got to see the manuscript. And they said to each other: 'After all, he did win the Booker, and we must do our best with this.' And so they attached a shiny sticker to the front cover saying 'From the author of *Life of Pi*' and they charged £15.99 for it, even though it was quite a small book, so that anyone who bought it would know it was literature. But alas, the reviewers cried in their hordes, 'Boo to Yann!' and 'Boy, does this one suck!' and 'What does he think he's doing?' And Yann went back to Canada, only not with such a large sack of money, to ponder the two great dangers of novel-writing, which are the difficulties of working with allegory and animals.

SOUTH OF THE RIVER

BLAKE MORRISON

Nat and Anthea sat in the Millennium Café, in sight of the London Eye, scanning the newspaper headlines about foot-and-mouth disease. Outside in the street the marchers protesting at the council's plans to build a new Tesco filed noisily by. Nat knew that in the end he would have an affair with her. The spirit of the age – that sense of bright, Blairite purpose – ordained it. In the meantime they would talk about literature.

'If you were writing a novel about the state of England in the period 1997–2002,' Anthea wondered, as the sound of *Definitely Maybe* erupted from the café's jukebox, 'what would you put in it?' 'Oh, I don't know,' Nat told her, 'the important thing is not to chuck in too many obvious symbols.' On the television screen above their heads, they could see David Beckham, prone on the carpet of green turf, flick his foot against an Argentine player. 'Too many lists of what people were listening to, or watching or reading.' He smoothed the pages of his copy of Nick Hornby's *About A Boy* with the fingers of his left hand. 'Or the kind of thing that was in the newspapers at the time. That tends to annoy people.'

'That reminds me,' she said, 'I had a lot of money invested in Equitable Life, and they say there's no compensation.' 'A pity,' he agreed, 'but about that novel. You should never blind readers with the depth of your research. I was out sailing the other day, by the way, and the bowsprit tacked amidships over the jib. Or something. On the other hand' – he paused to watch a giant badger emerge from a dustbin on the café's forecourt and go scuttling down the street – 'you do need an enduring image, an animal even, something that can thread its way through the plot and make a decent cover.'

'That's very interesting,' she said. 'But surely there are some issues that real people *would* have talked about at the time.' 'Oh certainly,' he said, 'but you need to strike a balance between the mundane drift of ordinary lives *and* the big events rolling on along the horizon. God, verrucas are hell. And I'm really upset about the Middle East.' 'I think I see,' she said, spilling a copy of the *Hello* Princess Diana memorial number out of her handbag.

'What about race?' 'Has to be there,' Nat assured her. 'Black character absolutely mandatory these days.' On the jukebox the strains of *Definitely Maybe* had given way to The Verve's *Bittersweet Symphony*. Outside the marchers had been replaced by a convoy of fuel protestors. 'And what about sex?' she asked. 'I thought you'd never ask,' he said.

Back at her flat, she arched hungrily above his flaccid body in a maelstrom of passion broken only by the sound of a motorcycle courier delivering their invitation to the Millennium Night party at the Dome . . . [*continues for 500 pages*].

FINAL DEMANDS

FREDERIC RAPHAEL

With a copy of his latest devastatingly brilliant screenplay, *About Myself, Once More*, pressed against the lapel of his suit, the famous novelist Adam Morris stepped across the yellow stripe and approached the immigration officer.

'Anything to declare?'

'Wilde always said that he had nothing to declare but his genius, didn't he? I suppose with me it's my genus. There may be subtler ways of acknowledging your Jewishness, of course. Some races make a virtue of their inconspicuousness. I suppose we're just inconspicuous about our virtues.'

'What brings you to America, Mr . . . uh . . . Morris?'

'Oh, I wouldn't say I was brought. Impelled, maybe, or perhaps only *pro*-pelled? It's a fine point. Like a biro. Though I'm more of a felt tip man myself. If I had any tip left to feel, that is, after a flight to LA. The journey as spiritual ether. Didn't Norman Mailer say that we leave our illusions behind in departures and pick them up again in arrivals?'

The immigration officer sank bank exhausted. Adam could see Rachel and her black friend waiting for him in the arrivals hall. She looked unimaginably beautiful and brilliant. The black friend was tall and black. Outside there was blue sky and white concrete. Descriptions were always the most boring part of novels, he thought. What people really liked was sparkling dialogue.

'Mr Raph . . . I mean, Mr Morris,' the black man said, shaking Adam's hand. 'You're one hell of a writer, sir.'

'Ah, assault and flattery. Wins out every time. Didn't Socrates say that we compliment the people we secretly dread? Or dread the people we secretly compliment? I can't remember. But then the only stamp on my passport's the state of Amnesia. Now, you must be my daughter.'

'Kierkegaard said that there is no "must".'

'But then Kierkegaard had never seen a rogue elephant, had he? Darling, you're so *chic* I could shriek. LA suits you. Symposia were always cosier in 90 degrees . . . Bill's dead, isn't he? You don't have to tell me.'

'Tales of the unexpected are always expected in the end, aren't they? Essentially determinist? Or maybe only determinedly essential. You know, when I saw him stretched out on the slab I thought of that line of Beckett's.'

'Sam, or Tom?'

'Sam. I know you've never liked him since he pipped you for the Prix Goncourt that time.'

'Waiting for God-awful, I know. But tell me about Bill?'

'Well, watching him lying there groaning I realised you were right when you said there's a fundamental difference between nostalgia and elegy.'

'Poor Bill. He should never have come to LA to hang out with all the goys. Did he have any last words?'

He said to me: 'Raitch – tell Fred . . . I mean Adam that he really is a genius. Not like dumb little also-ran me.'

'Bill said that? Oh, the vanity of the humiliated. You know, there's a kind of conceit in serial self-deprecation. Didn't Nietzsche once say that the only terrible thing about the play of life is that there are no *entr'actes*?' [*continues for thousands of pages*].

CONSTITUTIONAL

HELEN SIMPSON

Sometimes they talked in the car and sometimes they talked a lot.

'Mum?'

'Yes?'

'Am I allowed to say spermatozoa?'

'I don't see why not. Have you got your inhaler? And the cheque for the ski-trip?'

'*Mum.*'

He was the only one in the world who listened to her, Ariadne reflected, and did what she said. Not like Patrick, her husband, who lay in the bath worrying about his pension contributions. Misery was like a tree, she thought: the topmost branches might hang far above you, but they still had the capacity to fall on your head.

'I remember when I was at school,' she said, wondering what had happened to the Coldplay CD. 'My mind was full of girlish dreams, and the summer afternoons seemed to roll on for ever like the squares in a patchwork quilt. But now . . .'

'You're a loser, mum,' her daughter Tallulah

had told her the other day. 'Xanthe's mother's got a shop in Bruton Street selling designer jewellery, and Araminta's mum's having an affair with Pete Doherty.'

Sometimes the terrible struggle of the school, this merciless crawl through foul air and the black talons of malevolent rain, gave her, Ariadne, pause. The journey took forty-five minutes, forty-two if you took a devious left-hand turn along Murgatroyd Avenue, forty-six if you stalled at the roundabout.

'Mum,' said Toby again, from the back seat. 'Will you test me on my Hebrew?'

They turned right into the Finchley Road, past the shop that had those nice hanging baskets and the deli that did the goats' milk cheese.

'Mum,' said Tallulah. 'Can I have my nose pierced? Can I?'

It was so hard, Ariadne reflected, so nutritionless, this cramped bourgeois existence. Lying awake at night in your mid-terrace semi, negotiating the M25 in your BMW, pondering the landscape from the window of your *gîte* in the Dordogne, your mind ran away with you, constructed unappeasable phantoms for you to chase. And then you came awake to find the au pair had measles and the French windows were jammed shut. Stalled, stymied, silenced.

The school gates loomed, the 4X4s tussling before them like embattled dinosaurs. Silently the children disembarked. Deserted, she thought, abandoned, bereft. Suddenly Toby's face appeared at the window.

'Spermatozoa,' he said. 'Bye, mum.'

The brief, epiphanic moment hung above them in the dense and terrible sky.

ON BEAUTY

ZADIE SMITH

One may as well begin with Kiki in the delicatessen.

'What I need,' explained Kiki, hauling her mountainous two hundred and fifty pound African-American ass towards the counter, 'is a homey, warm, chunk-filled, pastry-lovin', finger-lickin', hot-doggety, down home kind of pie.' She recalled being invincible and truth-loving and twenty years old, and thinking that if she could only be honest about the kind of pie she wanted, then she could emerge moist-eyed in the light that would drench her and those around her in its languorous aura.

'Hey there,' said the brother behind the plastic sneeze-guard. 'Heeey there. Ain't I seen you some place before?'

'. . . A kind of back-porch kind of pie, do you know what I mean? Nothing sour . . . or sassy.'

'Sure I have. You been in one of them Zadie Smiths novel, sister.'

'I don't . . .'

'Yes you have. Can tell. First there's the way you speak quite ordinary sentences but sorta emphasis-

ing quite arbitrary words, kind of like you was com-
pensating for their dullness.'

'It ain't . . .'

'Sure it is. Pretty soon you'll start talking in
CAPITAL LETTERS, like it was some PRETTY
IMPORTANT THING you was wanting to say. Only
it AIN'T. Then, 'fore I know where I am, there'll be
some huge, multi-cultural family jes' sashaying in
from nowhere with names like Jerome 'n' Levi 'n'
Zora . . .'

'Hold on there . . .'

'And the whole structure just insisting on its
complex derivation from existing literary sources.
In this case, sister, Mr E. M. fuckin' Forster. I mean,
what is it about that girl? And her on the Man
Booker shortlist an' all.'

Suddenly, to her abstracted relief, Kiki found
that Jerome, Levi and Zora were collected in a
familial huddle at her side. She clutched them to
her, affixiating them in the quaint caverns of her
armpits.

'Yeah and I'll tell you some stuff about them. Like,
one of them'll really be into black street culture . . .'

('. . . Yo my man,' Kiki now heard Levi greet her,
as they swapped a bunch of high fives. 'Bin hangin'
with my homies in the hood is all.')

'. . . And check out the chick with the college
education, dropping some big fancy names . . .'

('. . . And I'm, like, saying to the poetry class,' Zora presently informed her mother, 'surely Foucault has negated all this')

'You hear what I'm saying, sister? Now, I knows it ain't easy for a girl to get herself in the newspapers every time she write a book. She gotta get herself looking real nice and have some fahn photograph that the editor of the *Daily Telegraph*'s gonna love. Like she was in Destiny's Child or something. But, believe me you got a difficulty . . .'

But Kiki had seen the pie, golden and in the centre a red and yellow compote of sticky baked fruit. She thought of her husband, weaselly white-guy Howard, and whether she had quite done loving him. Still she managed to raise her face again towards the sneeze-guard.

'What kinda difficulty?'

'Sister . . . It ain't my place to say so, but you're generic.'

'What so bad about that?'

The brother wrinkled his nose. 'Well, curiously enough, in this particular case, nuthin'. I mean, honey, you read the chick in the *Times Literary Supplement*? Where it say that "*On Beauty*'s most interesting ethical endeavour is the way it fits itself so perfectly – happily inhabiting its own apparent slightness"?'

'What that mean?'

'Seems to me it means "We have a problem here only I'm too polite to say so." But relax, honey, it ain't your fault you're campus-lite. Only it ain't gonna last for ever. Someone gonna see through the trick that girl playing, and then what, huh?'

Kiki exhaled vertiginously. 'At least I'll have the pie,' she said.

THE LIGHT OF DAY

GRAHAM SWIFT

. . . Rain outside again. Its hiss. The noise a crisp packet makes when you open it. That a biro makes when, regretfully, you lay it down. I notice things. He said that, once before. The agent. 'You notice things, Graham.'

'It's my job,' I said. 'Noticing things. I'm a writer. Take water, for instance. It's just melted ice.'

'That's good,' he said. 'I like that.' I could see his point. He knows what he likes, the agent. Maybe he likes what he knows, too. Like Genesis, in that song.

The agent. A man in an office. At the end of the Northern line. Outside, the rain again. April showers. Niagara Falls. I live in Wimbledon. After Putney. But before Raynes Park. You'll have been there. It's somewhere to write about. And in the early days I even liked walking round it. Leaving the house. Taking a stroll. Seeing the sights.

She puts her head round the door. 'Good day, love? Written much?'

A simple question. A simple question, that needs an answer. If we could answer all the questions, then they wouldn't need asking. It stands to reason.

'Ten words,' I say. 'Different ones, too. Some long ones. Some short ones. A couple of definite articles. A personal pronoun. It's a start. In a week there'll be a paragraph. In a few years – who knows? A short story? A novella even. I'm not counting. Words are like chickens. I know that much. You just don't count them.'

Then I stop. She goes away. Silence. It's the loudest sound on earth.

Sometimes fate steps in. You win some prizes. You get a lot of money. And then people start to want things. Always wanting things. Like the publisher. On the phone. Always ringing.

'Graham! Haven't heard from you in a while . . .'

Hasn't anyone told him? That it's a seven-year stretch. With no remission. And no visiting hours. That the words don't write themselves.

'Don't mind me,' he says, 'but you ought to get out more. That's what the critics say.'

'Forget it,' I say, above the noise of the humming, drumming, ruthless, sluiceless rain. 'What do they know? Less is more. More or less.'

TOMORROW

GRAHAM SWIFT

HELLO! I'm Paula and I'm the narrator of Graham Swift's new novel. If you've ever read any of Mr Swift's other novels then you'll already know a good bit about me. You'll know, for example, attentive geographer that you are, that I probably live in South London – in Putney, say, or Dulwich. And you'll have a good idea of the way in which Mr Swift renders my thought processes down on paper. That's right. Lots of thoroughly ordinary sentences, filtered through a thoroughly ordinary mind. The proof of the pudding is in the eating. You can take it or leave it. Now and again there comes a flourish – Sussex in the Sixties, the very phrase like a glistening salad – but mostly it's a succession of stock formulations. Sometimes I wonder whether this is actually a very exciting way of writing a novel, but then I'm not a successful novelist like Mr Swift. Anyway, beauty is in the eye of the beholder. And it's a watched pot that never boils. Oh dear me yes.

Well, Mr Swift has given me a little secret to divulge, as I lie here in the small hours in Putney or Dulwich or Wimbledon. Quite frankly I'd like to get to sleep, but you can't always get what you want, can you, and sometimes the thing you need escapes you (Mr Swift has this odd habit, you know, of saying the same thing in slightly different ways). Actually it's quite a big secret. Have I been cheating on my husband, Mike? Or has he been cheating on me? What is it that our twin children are going to find out tomorrow on their sixteenth birthdays? Well, that would be telling wouldn't it, and it would remove the whole element of suspense on which the averagely successful work of fiction depends.

No, I think I'd better string things out a bit. So I'll tell you about how Mike and I met, back at university in the 1960s, and Grandpa Pete, and Mike's thesis about snails, and our house in Herne Hill. And all the time you'll be wondering about what dreadful thing it is that I'm waiting to reveal to the children next morning, won't you? Except that Mr Swift has this other odd habit of always giving the game away long before the closing page. He did it in *The Light of the Day* and now he looks as if he's going to do it again in this one. There's nothing I can do to stop him. You win some, you lose some. Mumps are better than measles. *Après moi le deluge.* Oh well, here goes. Mike was infertile, you see, and the children were hatched out of a test-tube.

So now you know what awaits them, Nick and

Kate, in the pale morning as the first stray light of Midsummer glows evanescently over the parched and friable grass – another flourish there, I trust you noticed. And yet I can't help thinking that it's only page 153 and most novels go on a lot longer than this. They do, though. Never mind. It would be a shame to stop now, and I don't think Mr Swift's publishers would be very pleased. So perhaps I'd better tell you about Otis our cat, and how terribly upset we all were when he disappeared, and the affair I had with the vet. His capable forearms. His rolled sleeves. You don't miss these things. Oh and a three-page description of a posh hotel we stayed in would certainly move matters forward a bit.

Nearly dawn, now. I must confess – it's not something I'd ever say in public, not when there are people about – that I worry about Mr Swift. I mean, he can really write rather brilliantly sometimes, but for some reason the bits where he does this don't sound like me, which is a bit of a disappointment for a girl. What a clever person would call *compromising the integrity of the narrative voice*. All the same, though, I got quite excited at the prospect of the final scene. What will the children say when they find out their origins lie not in daddy here but in a phial of anonymous sperm?

Wait a minute, though, it's light! It jolly well is! It's already getting light and here we are on the final page! Now, I don't know anything about novels, but it strikes me that there's something a bit weird going on. There is, though. I always thought that if you spent all those chapters, all those carefully marshalled words, all those patient accretions of sentences, building up to a denouement then you owed it to the reader to actually *have* the denouement rather than just stop at the moment where things are supposed to get interesting. Oh well. Mr Swift won the Booker Prize once, and I'm sure he knows best.

POLITICS

ADAM THIRLWELL

Hello!

My name is Adam Thirlwell. Although I am quite young, I have been thinking very seriously about the nature of comedy. I would like to share these thoughts with you.

A lot of people do not properly understand about comedy, I think.

COMEDY IS . . . NAUGHTY!

Perhaps some of you are not agreeing with me at this point. Perhaps you are thinking, 'I like Jane Austen and she is not naughty.' Well, comedy is naughty and it is not naughty. This is called a paradox.

In my novel *Politics*, Moshe and his friends Nana and Anjali are naughty. They do boysex. They do girlsex. They have longlovesexy kisskiss. When they are not having longlovesexy kisskiss they eat pizza and go shopping.

But they are serious people, I am thinking. Just because they only have longlovesexy kisskiss, eat pizza and go shopping does not mean they are not serious people.

Or that I am not a serious novelist.

Oh no.

COMEDY IS . . . DIFFICULT?

But what kind of comedy am I?

Well, I am a bit Martin Amis *Rachel Papers* era comedy and a bit Alain de Botton when he used to write fiction comedy, but mostly I am *faux-naif* comedy.

What is *faux-naif* comedy, you are asking? Well, it is lots of short, child-like sentences ('I think you are going to like Moshe. His girlfriend's name is Nana. I think you are going to like her too') but obviously written by a very brainy person who has read, for example, the work of the French writer Stendhal.

Stendhal is a very serious and important writer.

But it is not perhaps appropriate to mention him here.

COMEDY IS ABOUT . . . FUNNY DIALOGUE!

When they are not eating pizza (it is nice pizza and very reasonably priced) or doing longlovesexy kisskiss, Mishe and Nana and Anjali (and Nana's papa, the banker – I think you are going to like him too) talk to each other.

Maybe I need to be precise about how they talk to each other.

You see, when Nana says, 'You don't mind, do

you?' I put down, 'You don mind dyou?' And when Moshe asks her if she wants water I put down, 'Dyou wan water?' Later they visit a 'restron'.

This is not, of course, how people really talk.

But it is funny.

COMEDY IS . . . READING LISTS

As I said, I am serious comedy. Where I live at All Souls College, Oxford, there is a big, big library. Sometimes I am allowed to read the books. One of them is by a man named Gramsci. I like Gramsci. He says there is a thing called hegemony, which is 'the combination of force and consent, which balance each other reciprocally, without force predominating excessively over consent.' Moshe, Nana and Anjali are an example of hegemony, I am thinking.

Well, they had better be.

Or this would not be a serious novel!

And Mr Franklin from the publishers (I think I am going to like Mr Franklin) will be wanting his money back.

Reprinted with kind permission from the Guardian.

SUNDAY AT THE CROSS BONES

JOHN WALSH

'Think, John!' The voice in my ear buzzed like one of the metaphors from my no-holds barred report from the world crab-racing championships at Skegness. '*Think!*'

I could handle it, I told myself. Naturally the job of chief associate editorial honcho at the *Indescribably-boring* had its tensions. After all, those in-depth interviews with Elle Macpherson, those poignant accounts of what happened when the fire alarm went off at the King's Lynn Literature Festival, didn't write themselves. And now here I was, just back from composing a wide-ranging think-piece about spring hemlines to a top-level meeting with my all-too-fragrant editor, Fruitella.

'It's no good, John. What your literary career needs is continuity. Say what you like about Sebastian and that other lot you're always showing off with on the radio, but at least they keep churning them out. It's eight years now since you wrote that book claiming you were Irish.'

'*The Falling Angels*,' I fondly confirmed. 'Bejasus, yes, you adorable spalpeen. And really don't you think that pashmina might profitably drop just a *little* more off the shoulder?"

'It's called a cardigan, John. And it's at least four years since the book where you pretended your life was entirely governed by what you saw at the cinema.'

'*Are You Talking To Me?*' I eagerly glossed.

'That one. I hate to say this, John – it's something we only suggest to our authors when Waterstone's have stopped answering the phone – but have you ever thought of writing a novel?'

'Anyone can write a novel,' I coyly quipped. 'And tell me, is there a *Mr* Fruitella?'

'You're not anyone, John, that's the problem. But let's give it a go. History's in just now. Why not pick some historical figure people have just about heard of and write him up?'

'The Rector of Stiffkey,' I breathed, 'was a very interesting man. Torn between the duties of the cloth and the pleasures of the flesh. A kind of metaphor,' I extemporised, 'for the neuroses of the inter-war era.'

'Wasn't he the one who picked up tarts and got his head chewed off by a lion?' For once Fruitella looked interested. 'I should leave out the neuroses of the inter-war era and just concentrate on the tarts.'

'Done.' Breathlessly I texted my ever-encouraging editor, Simon, with the news. Almost immediately the phone rang.

'John. Is that you, mate?'

'Simon! I take it the idea of a three-month sabbatical to write my novel meets with your august approval?'

'Sorry, John, but apparently Pan's People are reforming. At least that's what it says in the *Guardian*. I told them that seeing it's a culture piece we'd get our best man round . . .' [*continues*].

THE STONE GODS

JEANETTE WINTERSON

Gosh, I've invented a new world!

I have, though. A whole new planet. Up there in the slanting, searing, horizon-hugging sky. What's it like? This isn't a work of realism, so let's just say that it has twigs as big as catamarans and elephants that trumpet through tea-kettles. Chocolate bars, dark as the soil, each the weight of an exploding galaxy. Or something.

There are a lot of capital letters in all this. M, for instance. M is for Massive, as in advance.

Hello, my name is Billie Crusoe. Yes, I *know* that comes from Defoe. Let's have another letter – I, for example, as in Inter-textual, or even B, as in Borrowed. Up here on Planet Blue I end up having sex with a lady robot called Spike. What happens? Well, the world is dark, and dark is the world. The strange thing about strangers is that you don't know who they are. She is my mouse-mat, the extra-strong mint that sets my torpid tongue aflame. Together we lurk, enmeshed, on the humid cusp of the world, marionettes teetering at the volcano's endangering edge . . . [*continues*]. Another useful letter is D, as in Dangerously overwritten.

But I haven't told you about poor old clapped-out planet earth and all the technology that keeps it going. This includes *Beatbots*, which are a kind of cyber-traffic warden and *Nifties*, which scuttle about under the floorboards and fix your heating. Jolly clever of me to think them up, don't you agree? So let's have Q, which is for Quite good jokes, sometimes. Oh, and there are *Jeanies*, those rather irritating female novelists who over-dosed on people like Italo Calvino and Angela Carter when young and keep ruining perfectly good ideas with rather obvious digressions on the nature of storytelling. They pop up all over the place.

I thought I'd just drop in a bit of personal baggage here, and include a page or two about the manuscript of this being found on a tube-train, just like mine was when some dim little editor person at Hamish Hamilton left her bag behind her on the seat. It was in all the papers, you know.

What are stories? Stories are like roads. Sometimes they go on all straight for miles, and sometimes they have bendy-bits like coat-hangers that take you where you'd least expect. Like things with no endings, they are endless. Once upon a time there was a novelist called Jeanette, a poor girl whom all the world loved until she started writing books that were all basically the same, full of descriptions that didn't describe anything, lesbian high-jinks on the forest floor and time's snow-white clouds rolling endlessly away. This one is about saving the planet, by the way, so let's end with an R, as in Recycling.

THE BOOK AGAINST GOD
JAMES WOOD

We spent our wedding night in a country hotel of quite egregious desuetude. We were too late for dinner, but room service sent up a mixed grill, brumous in aspect, and some subtly unstructured sandwiches. Jane ran the bath, while divesting herself of various abstruse undergarments. Behind her, steam rose in quaintly Niagaran fashion from the taps. I touched her anguished elbow.

'Doesn't Schopenhauer have a mad but really quite likeable theory that marriage corresponds to the chromatic possibilities of the pianoforte: engagement a cascade of vigorous arpeggios, wedding night a *crescendo*, old age plaintive *diminuendo* and so forth?'

Jane laughed. 'Darling, is this your way of asking me to commit osculation?'

'I was thinking about the vicar's address. I really couldn't stand the Reverend Mulcaster's pseudo-Dosteoveskyan line of argument. It seemed so fucking unempirical.'

Silently we climbed into the bed and uncoiled

ourselves amidst its punitive pillows. Without warning a phial of the purest provincial atavism broke in my hand and released an odiferous exaltation. 'Darling,' I said, 'something very important has happened. I've just decided that I don't believe in God.'

'How thrilling for you, my love. But can you not sleep?'

Wasn't it Heidegger who said that wakefulness was like sleep but without the pyjamas? Sadly the reference books that might have verified this discreet epigram were not to hand. Quietly we nestled together. Stroking her embarrassed shoulder, I knew that an agreeable consequence of our matrimonial state would be the necessity to read Nietzsche to her.

Meanwhile it was growing late. 'Darling,' she said mistily at one point. 'If you rolled over there would be just a little more space.'

'Oh no,' I replied seriously. 'Not more space, surely? Just less of it occupied.'

PLANET AMIS

PLANET AMIS

THE PREGNANT WIDOW

MARTIN AMIS

Keith Nearing – little Keith – lingered horizontally pool-side under the molten Italian sun. In the middle distance, yet still stratospherically far off, jet trails sped like weary spermatozoa. That molten Italian sun, plonked up there in the cerulean firmament like some fucking fried egg or other, had plans for Keith. Plans for him it had. Keith-plans. Keith-schemes. Beside him, Lily stirred one of her horrifying, *spatulate* legs, picked up his copy of *Bleak House*, ran a delicate pinkie along its spine and, coyly, said:

'Has Esther Summerson fucked anyone yet?'

'I don't think so. I'd have noticed if she had.'

'What about Lady Dedlock? Has she fucked anyone? Apart from Sir Lester, that is?'

'Lady Dedlock? Bound to have. I mean, Esther Summerson is her daughter, right?'

It was odd, Keith reflected, squinting sideways at Lily's torso, those moistly hub-capped hummocks damp beneath the scalloped veil of her bikini, how things worked out. This was the third time he'd turned up in one of Martin Amis's novels. First he'd been a malignant dwarf in the one about burned-out hippies. Then he'd been in the one about darts (or was it the Bomb – he couldn't remember.) Now, he seemed to be in one about the debilitating effects of the late '60s sexual revolution. But you could never tell.

'I heard,' Lily said, 'that when Terpsichore's boyfriend turns up – Zit, or Fraggle or whatever his name is – she's going to rub cottage cheese into her tits and then sort of *squidge* them all over him for an hour before they . . .'

That was another thing about being in a Martin Amis novel, Keith thought: everyone had silly names. Soon Calliope and Esperanza would arrive for tea and *soixante-neuf* by the fountain. Still, he knew, the vital statistics obsessed him: Calliope's proud 38–22–36; Esperanza's vertiginous 44–24–32; Lily's 60–60–60. No, that was the darts novel, surely?

Lily had gone off to the banqueting hall to brood about feminism. Out of the corner of his eye, he could see the small guy with the leather waistcoat and the scurfy rug conning over his scribble-pad.

'Hey you!' he found himself shouting. Shouting he found himself. 'You there! Mart or whatever your fucking name is. Why are you always here?'

'Did I say anything?' the small guy wondered.

'No, but it's always the same isn't it? Calliope,

Esperanza, Lily, that midget Italian Count or whoever he is – we don't really exist, do we? The only thing that really goes on in your books is you being really fucking clever.'

'You know, Keith,' Mart nodded, 'you're not as dim as I thought. Not at all. One day, you know – not soon, but one day – I'll give you something you want. Not girls with big tits and unimaginable sexual appetites but something you *really* want. Know what it is?'

'No,' Keith found himself whispering brokenly. The birds – those pertinacious pigeons and trite thrushes – were trilling their avian aria. 'I don't know.'

'Plausibility . . . Hey,' Mart sang. 'You'd better buzz over to the lawn now. This is a novel about the sexual revolution, right, and I hear Calliope's just taken her bra off.'

And Keith – little Keith, thrice-blessed Keith – buzzed.

MARTIN AMIS:
THE BIOGRAPHY
RICHARD BRADFORD

FROM THE INTRODUCTION

I am extremely grateful to Martin Amis, whose God-given genius should be instantly apparent to any lover of modern literature, for graciously allowing me to write this book. I should also like to thank his wife, the immensely stylish and intelligent Isabel Fonseca, author of several remarkable books herself, for her generous insistence that she should provide help with preparation of the work. I am especially indebted to Mr Amis's legal team, with whom my own lawyers enjoyed a number of long and fruitful conversations, and whose many helpful suggestions I have made a point of including in the text. [*Will this do?* – R. B.]

CHILDHOOD AND EARLY YEARS

The second son of a womanising, neurotic drunk, whose serial adulteries caused his first wife untold misery and whose negligent attitude to his children's upbringing led him virtually to abandon them in their mid-teens, Martin remains unfailingly loyal to his father's memory. 'I had an idyllic childhood,' he tersely informs me. 'Dad always had time to spare for me, taught me everything I knew and was an infallible rock and support. Do I make myself clear?' 'Certainly you do, Mr Amis,' I remarked, as I hurried to switch off the tape recorder.

ON HIS SUBJECT'S EMOTIONAL LIFE . . .

In the second week of January 1975, having reached a parting of the ways with his current girlfriend the Hon. Fruitilla Starborgling, elder daughter of Earl Twinch, to whom his second novel, *Bum Farts*, is charmingly dedicated, and pausing only for a brief dalliance with the fragrant Natalia Gorgon (plausibly identified by a remote acquaintance of Martin's I met in the Groucho as 'Smeggy' in *Yobs in Space*) whose memoir *Bastards Who Have Dumped Me* later caused such a sensation, and a possible encounter with Miss Mandy Miggins, proprietress of the Fancy Rat Café, Westbourne Grove, Martin then set his cap at the Zuleika of her generation, Miss Anastasia Bargs. I am delighted to report that Martin's legal team have no objection to a friend of Ms Bargs's being quoted to the effect that: 'Annie said she was devastated when he chucked her, but really, you know, he was so cool and gracious about it that in the end she was quite flattered. And then of course he put her in *Cunning Stunts* as . . . [*continues*].

ON THE CRISIS OF THE MID-1990S . . .

It is not for me to suggest that Martin's abandonment of his first wife, Antonia Phillips, for another woman is strongly reminiscent of his father's behaviour thirty years before, or that the parallels between the sexual behaviour of father and son are so striking that no prudent biographer could ignore them. No indeed: no topic could be of less interest to me. Yet by 1993 it was clear to informed observers that the marriage was on the rocks. The distinguished literary journalist John Walsh, who attended Amis's Oxford college some years after he left it and once glimpsed the back of Ms Phillips's head as she walked into the Ivy, recalled seeing them together at the Cheltenham Literary Festival: 'You could tell it was all over. She had a Coke. He ordered a lemon juice. The body chemistry was way out.'

Unhappily, the split coincided with Amis's decision to dispense with the services of his long-term literary agent, who by a cruel irony was married to his old friend Julian Snargs. Alas that the law of copyright does not allow me to quote from Snargs's accusatory letter! But I am reliably informed by Mr Christopher Hitchens, without whose unbelievably tactless indiscretions this book could not have been written, that the exact words were: *Mart you treacherous swine. I hope you rot in hell for this, you bastard. That's the last time we ever play snooker.*

CONCLUSION: IS HE A GREAT WRITER?
Well, it depends on what you mean by 'great' [*continues for dozens of pages*].

THE LIFE OF
KINGSLEY AMIS
ZACHARY LEADER

. . . Opinions differed as to Amis's precise emotional state at this time. Barry Refill, a lifelong friend from the Garrick Club, maintained that 'He was a real gentleman to the last. I mean, if he'd had six gin-and-tonics he'd go on and drink a seventh if you bought it for him. That was the kind of man he was.' A dinner with the novelist Julian Barnes, however, displayed this titanic literary figure in less flattering light. Amis arrived, to quote Barnes, 'in a not terribly good mood'. Offered a glass of Château Mouton-Rothschild 1953 he flung the bottle on the floor with a shout of 'This wine's piss' before asking his host, 'I suppose you're writing some fucking book aren't you?' The conversation then moved on to address the situation in apartheid-era South Africa. 'Basically, we need to line all the niggers up against the wall and shoot them,' Amis deposed before collapsing in a pile of vomit. Barnes admitted that the evening 'really wasn't what you might call a success'.

In a later conversation with an earlier biographer about whom I shall attempt to be scrupulously fair, Amis attempted to rationalise these pronouncements. 'Basically we need to line all the niggers up against a wall and shoot them' meant 'I am afraid the prospect of Mr Mandela's release is somewhat remote.' 'I suppose you're writing some fucking book aren't you?' meant 'I am looking forward very much to your new work.' Amis also maintained that he threw the bottle of wine on the floor 'in an attempt to disable the large number of green phosphorescent serpents I had seen writhing there.'

Much of this trauma is reflected in *Women I Bloody Hate Them*, which, while no less funny than its predecessor *I Want A Shag*, is a more challenging work. Several critics have detected an autobiographical element in this story of a serial adulterer with a drink problem who . . . [*continues for thousands of pages*].

NORTHANGER ABBEY: A SCREENPLAY

MARTIN AMIS

Scene: Bath, exterior, day. Wind ceaselessly crazes the frightening trees, etc. A carriage bowls friskily into view. Within, Miss Catherine Morland and friend, in torpid transit.

MISS M: (*pertly adjusts bonnet*): How do I look?

FRIEND: Babelocious.

MISS M: (*inspects cleavage*): Jesus! If this doesn't drag the animal to the party I'll freak. Period.

FRIEND: Tilney? He's cool. But, like, insane. And the old guy – is he ever weird?

MISS M: Whatever. You like Britney Spears best, or Celine Dion?

(*They amuse themselves playing whist or some other pretty period diversion. CUT TO Northanger Abbey. Bats privily prowl. Deer surreptitiously stalk, etc.*)

GENERAL TILNEY: This chick Morland, is she pissing me off or what?

TILNEY: The *fuck*?

GENERAL TILNEY: There's no bread. I made them run a computer check. Plus she reckons I offed your ma. Does that sound like a good deal?

TILNEY: You're breaking my heart, Dad.

GENERAL TILNEY: You young guys got no respect.

(*They arm wrestle playfully on carpet. Butler, housemaids etc. look raptly on. CUT TO Morland household, exterior, night. Ring at door.*)

MISS M: This better be good, buster.

TILNEY (*insinuatingly*): Your pa home?

MISS M: Writing some asshole sermon is all. So . . . do I get to date you at the Prom or what?

TILNEY: Just as soon as I get out of rehab, hon.

MISS M: Fuckin' *A*!

(*They embrace as a file of cheerleaders marches behind. Profiles in all newspapers, Amis wins Oscar etc.*)

POETRY CORNER

KILLING TIME

SIMON ARMITAGE

This is the kind of poem that people like to read these days, combining street-wise references with post-modern tricks

It's the kind of thing that gets put on Channel Four with Christopher Eccleston my name is Simon, I'm thirty-six.

This is a poem about the Millennium, and by extension the whole meaning of existence, I'm dropping in as much stuff from the *Guardian* news pages as I can think of and you highbrows can keep your distance.

Meanwhile on the Thames, the people trying to hoist the BA London Eye are all shagged out,

This kind of thing is supposed to make poetry dead contemporary, but you know I have my doubts.

While on deck the waiters clear the muddied plates, while hoping that no one will fall in

With any luck this book will be warmly commended in next week's *Observer* by Mr Tom Paulin.

Water laps against each prow. It's the eve of the dawn, a millennium lately departed
It's no good you thinking, 'That Simon, he'll stop now for sure', cos I've only just started.

And finally, in a West Yorkshire village a poet delivers himself of his burden
I've an idea I've seen this kind of stuff somewhere before in – could it be – the *Collected Works* of W. H. Auden?

THE DEATH OF KING ARTHUR

SIMON ARMITAGE

You who are listeners and love lightly to learn
Of the practitioners of poetry and their awesome
   advances
Hither haply hurry, and hist to my tale of the
   travails of Simon,
And his search, amidst much that was passingly
   modish,
For a suitable subject. 'Miss Oswald has done well'
Our bard ruminated, 'with her rhapsodic Homeric
   re-stylings.
My own *Sir Gawain* was most suavely saluted and
   critically
Commended. Yes, history's the thing, and King
   Arthur my
Lyrical lode-star.' And with that he boldly began,
   his journey commencing,
In prudent preparation, with the quest for a style.
   'Malory won't do'
He crisply concluded. 'Too Greenery-yallery,
   quintessentially quaint.

No, I shall follow that poem in Lincoln Cathedral
     library,
Antique and alliterative, though Tennyson it ain't.
     When these
Deeds were done he dubbed his knights and dealt out
Dukedoms in different lands. How does that sound?
     For the poet's realm
Has many mansions, in this proud, post-modernist
     time.
And to the dismal dearth of scansion may be aptly
     added
The lamentable lack of rhyme. But never mind.
     They were fast
In fording to the fine coast of Normandy. You know, I
     think I'm
On to something here. Mistress Duffy wastes her
     words in adumbrating
Odes for textbooks; Sir Andrew Motion's muse is
     mostly maladroit. At Sir
Geoffrey one looks listlessly askance. Yet hearken
     here to
Sir Simon, poesy pricked on the pin-point
Of his *ersatz*-Arthurian lance.

TON UP FOR WYSTAN!

*(Lines in celebration of the centenary of the
birth of W. H. Auden)*

He buggered off in the dead of winter
The Nazis were in Poland, the Czechs had been
    smothered
Not quite the time for a poetic gesture
The country was at war; no one much bothered
Even the most fervent well-wisher would
Wonder why he'd flown the coop with Isherwood

Far from his agreeable boat-trip
The armies ran over the Maginot Line
The smoke rose, and the burned bodies were raked
    into particles
But his sojourn in the Big Apple was marked
By a number of magazine articles

Now he's in every broadsheet in the country
And all that equivocal stuff about Spain is 'the
    conscience of a nation' –
Rather than the usual cry of self-preservation

The thoughts of a dead man, turned all
     transcendent
Make a nice 1500 words in the *Independent*
'We must love one another and die.'
Sounds good, Uncle Wiz. Let's give it a try.

Guild of poets, stifle sniggers
Wystan Auden's reached three figures
Let the English vessel lie
Safe beneath Manhattan sky

On the far side of the Atlantic
Let the poet's muse stay antic
Never mind absconding sods
Keep the free man from false Gods . . .

HUMAN CHAIN

SEAMUS HEANEY

AN IRISH POET FORESEES HIS DESTINY
(AFTER W. B. YEATS)

A grand auld life it is, to be sure
Being an Irish poet
Your subjects ready-made
Like the warm soda-bread on Mrs McCavity's
    window-sill
Robbed by us Fenian boys on our dawn parade
And your critics – Muldoon and Toibin and the
    others –
Lined up in the *Guardian Review*, like the Catholic
    band of brothers
To offer their benedictions. No half measures in
Our world, are there spalpeens? Just solidarity. Like
    O'Grady's bar
In downtown Ballymaclutch, a full pint for everyone,
The Guinness flowing pure like milk from the
    Virgin's breast,
The least lyrical among us given his crutch.
    A grand auld
Life to be sure.

FONS ET ORIGO (CF. AENEID VII, 94, CONTINUED)
Ah, Derry, Derry, risen out of the bog
Forged in the raging furnace of Tir-na-Nog
Priest-blessed, nun-haunted, the Pope gazing down
From the scullery wall, my grandfather's false teeth,
Marinading in Steradent, the goose-feather
    eiderdown
Bought that time in Roscommon, at the traveller's fair
All swept aside by the summons to London,
And the boat from Rosslare.

GENEALOGY
Who is this coming up to Queen Square
Flint-eyed Hibernian peasant?
To join Wystan and Tom, Ez and the rest
Elegiac, but effervescent
All sweat-lustrous and bedewed, the elderflower
In the glare of the noon-day sun
No, you can't write like that in London N1.

BALLYBUNION ECLOGUE
Those evenings when we'd just wait and watch
And fish, the rod wound back inch by inch on its
    spool,
Looking for the symbols that Irish poems are
    crammed with,
That metaphor that would clinch it, have the guy
    at the
TLS sit up on his stool. And see, as if by magic,

The otter's head appear in the flow, dark among
    the midge-drifts, the river's glue
The swell of old Ireland, its dead souls lost on the
    flood tide . . . [*continues*]
'I'll take the otter,' I yelled. 'What about you?' Poor
    Paidraig, all
That was left (I'd previously had the beached trout
    and the silver stone
We'd found at the wayside too) was old Mr
    McGarrigle's field of spring wheat,
He of the Gabolga, full of shadow, I grant you,
The shrike's beak piercing the field mouse's skull
But it just wouldn't do.

HE REMEMBERS MULLHOLLANDSTOWN

Carpet-crawlers in convent lace, the old red trace of the earth tied

Up in grass knots, brass pots cast aside in the hedge's loosestrife-striven

Shadow. And the horse's spavined forelock, swollen like

Church coffers at Christmas. Meltwater, foxbreath, shankscrimbler, a past

Interred in madeupwords. Snow spread across the dead pasture

Like a bridal train, and down in the snicket-sanctioned streamlet

Those otters (again).

FINE FELLERS, ALL OF THEM
In long trousers that stopped at mid-calf
We read our catechisms with Father O'Hoolahan,
    chased tennis balls
Our fathers farmed fields, made wills, played at
    shinty
Our mothers stayed home, talked and sewed,
    anchorites all.

Patrick O'Rourke's at Ennis, in the hotel trade
Young Connor, in silk, prowls the courts
Coughlan made Maynooth too hold to him
I write poems – it's a living, of sorts.

THE BOOK OF MY ENEMY: COLLECTED VERSE 1958–2003
CLIVE JAMES

A LETTER TO MR CLIVE JAMES, TO MARK THE PUBLICATION OF HIS *COLLECTED VERSE*

Dear Clive, I took your book up to the study
The better to appraise you next your peers
Martin, Craig Raine, Larkin – all those fuddy-duddies
That you've addressed your poems to for years
Such coy encomia might be thought romantic
A better word, alas, is 'sycophantic'.

Your verse, of course, depends on incongruity
Those brainy thoughts hemmed in by metric bands
The reader may find only superfluity
A poet rarely sitting on his hands
Using the dreary plod of terza rima
To hymns his jaunts to Tokyo and Lima.

'To Gore Vidal at 50' – you're fond of anniversaries
And bustling round the globe as cultural gaucho

Your chums bag TV shows and bursaries
In a land where Wood Lane meets the Groucho
You pastiche Amis (K) with effervescence
In a style a few yards short of obsolescence.

It's not all bad – oh no, there's personal stuff in here
Things about love, truths uttered from beneath the
      moral hat
The only absentee is Germaine Greer
Amid a throng of Ozzie takes on where it's at
'81, your rhyming round-up says, was quite a year
Two decades on, the SDP seem smallest of small
      beer.

'Last night the sea dreamed it was Greta Scacchi'
I'll admit I giggled hugely over that
Styled like an elephant with howdah by Versace
A versifying fizz that's fallen sadly flat.
My own credentials won't match up to you – alas
I never wrote for Ian Hamilton's *Review*.

Oh well. I have to go now Clive, my pen runs idle
Unlike your own uncurbed extravaganzas
Unchained by any editorial bridle
And dancing on from stanza unto endless stanza
As for your talent – well I'll gladly tender that
There are three Clives – James I, James II and
      Old Pretender.

HOW BOILETH YE POT

ANDREW MOTION

A new 'civic liturgy' on the theme of St George

Hark how this patented late-Romanticism of mine,
with its dying falls – ah, that torrent of melting
silver,
the rain on the forest floor, the clouds carved in
the shape of the bear's
dread paw – and its undemanding half-rhymes, so
zealously persists. Yet for a man in my position –
the Laureateship
gone, the *Guardian* not what it was – such prestige
commissions
are hard to resist. But that reminds me. The poem.
What should it
say? Who is this fellow, a pilgrim, that symbol of
spirit and nation,
who swerves off alone from the far-flung field of
folk? Whence came their
desperate alliteration? What better way to greet
the Shakespeare Institute's
kind suggestion than a host of unanswerable
questions? But that reminds me again. Well no, it
doesn't remind

me at all – this is a poetic device – yet what, I ask
of you,
is this country summoned to be and to become?
And what is he called, this
elemental wanderer, who forsakes the forest for
the city, where
the runcible spoons of state have beaten his eggs
into new
omelettes? One thing you will notice about these
poems of
mine, for better or worse, is that as they continue
they stop being what most people would regard as
poetry and turn
into prose, neatly chopped up into lines of
irregular blank
verse. And here is our pilgrim, on the world's
latest threshold,
bright axe newly-minted. The greatest mystery
facing us now
is how to keep faith – that, and how on earth this
kind of thing
still gets printed. Let me say it again. How to keep
going? How to press on?
Here in the field where sinuous rills unwind,
tenebrous yet time-bright,
and clouds that are forged in the shape of
something or other announce
another most heartening return to the limelight.

IN THE BLOOD

ANDREW MOTION

Bliss was it in that bright dawn to be alive,
Mummy's step on the parched lawn (O my hot
youth!)
The lanes of genteel Oxfordshire, bat-haunted
night
gaunt in the hedgerows, misery handed down,
along
With words one couldn't say (like 'toilet'
'serviette' and 'Strewth')
Oh how the perilous trail ran on, a trifle sadly
To the terrifying public school at Radley.
An English education – alas, it made me what I
am –
feet shuffling on gymnasium floor, coleoptera,
Spam.
And thence to glorious Oxford – my park, my
pleasaunce,
and that scree of words come tumbling raptly o'er
the
vertiginous cliffs (*I say, this is rather good,
isn't it? A. M.*)

to mark the end of adolescence, knowing that I would
Hull-wards hearken, to blithely drench myself in scent
Of Larkin. How long ago it seems, how long? The bard
Of Humber one and twenty years a gone! Much else besides.
Footloose and fancy free – the poet's sempiternal ruse,
I have at least been faithful to my muse.
She of the royal birthday, she of the foreign war,
She of the state occasion and the Whitehall door!
The needle hovers high upon the reminiscent graph
My agent's sold an extract to the *Daily Telegraph.*

MOY SAND AND GRAVEL

PAUL MULDOON

Being a distinguished contemporary Irish poet –
like Seamus and
Tom and them other fellers –
carries its own responsibilities. Bringing in the
cultural allusions
(Tom likes Verlaine, I'm more of a Valery guy)
while remembering in the end
that your verse man, like the one who recited to
Brian Boru,
is only a story teller. It
doesn't have to scan, of course, but you
can arrange it over the page to look
as if it
does. And meanwhile the funny place-names
need a mention,
so I'm putting in Auchnacloy, Cullaville and
Derrymacash, some of
them
in *italics*, in the hope that
they'll grab your attention. Did I forget anything?
Oh

yes Dev and O'Hanlon and all that ould Gaelic
stuff. That fifties childhood, of course,
with the packet of fags on the car seat and the
clothes built to
last. Anything else would be
forswearing our past. Me, Seamus, Tom and the
others. As poetry
goes – and boy does it go – we're just calling your
bluff.

THE WASTE OF SPACELAND

CRAIG RAINE

So here's a book about Tom
Who, in a very real sense, we all hail from
Yes, me and old Seamus, Muldoon and the others.
The whole sodding modern poetic *galère*
That gets its advances from the chaps at Queen Square
That chittering band of post-modern blood brothers.

But Tom now, what an influence
On yours truly – not unduly, some might say, the
    old boy's
Criterion not quite the machete I wield
In *Areté*. Prufrock at half-cock?
Less of that, buster.
He didn't trust her, his first wife, that is,
When she went tonto.
If their love was ethereal, then he lived his material.
And got out pronto.

In the room the students come and go
Talking of their tutor's libido.

I was a Martian once. I wrote a postcard home

From a lifetime's wandering on the Oxford loam
Glittering prizes – I'll take all they're giving
Teaching students? Well, it's a living.

But back to Tom, who wrote of wastelands, knew
      Virginia and Leonard,
And criticised the critic, and was a mite too
Pacific if you ask me, never went off
In a huff. As for me, show me the bastards who
      dump on my
Stuff and I'll soon have a go. Especially the sods at
Front Row. Anyway, you might think
Tom here was a dry old stick. Actually, no.
Take it from me he was a real goer, married a chick
      forty years
His junior, danced like a dervish so they say,
      couldn't have
Been spoonier. Never mind the worries about the
      fully
Lived life. You should just see Tom go with his
      spanking new
Wife.

(Not a point, alas, that I much care to labour
– the lady's a shareholder at Faber & Faber.)

I could have been a coiled serpent under a log
But settled for Art and a soft college job.

THE OXFORD
MANNER

FLOURISHING:
LETTERS 1928–1946
ISAIAH BERLIN: Edited by Henry Hardy

All Souls, Oxford, 1 July 1936

TO THE HON VENETIA STARBORGLING[1]

Dear Boffles,

I feel acute guilt & displeasure at having left the postage stamp that I borrowed from you some months ago, while staying at your very nice house in Hampshire,[2] unreturned, the thought of having prevailed upon your essential goodness, fine nature, elegance of judgment &c being sufficient to plunge me into a gloom unrelieved by various events of whose relative magnitude I leave you to judge.

1. There is a civil war in Spain. This is really very serious.
2. Sammy's[3] non-elevation to the professorship of Greek. How this came, or did not come, about, is a source of cataclysmic misery,

for we had done everything in our power, written to Frisk and Whiskers[4] about it &c. And Sammy – so mad & gay & snobbish & sweet & so disappointed. Hearing of his arch-rival Professor Vole's victory in the election – a learned, scholarly, unsuitable man – I at once rushed off to dine with him, & I think really consoled him by my insistence that it is the striking, original figures who survive in Oxford legend irrespective of whether they do any work or not.

3. Bobby's[5] failure in Greats. This, I must admit, perplexed me gravely. He had done a fine Latin translation and a noble Greek unseen. While his inability to attend Schools for the final three papers undoubtedly counted against him, one would have thought his qualities of gentlemanliness and sympathetic understanding, not to mention his father's very agreeable residence in Perthshire, where I stayed last summer, would have redeemed him to some extent in the examiner's eyes . . . [continues].

1 The Hon Venetia Starborgling (1913–84) daughter of Lord Dull, Minister for Agriculture, February to March 1925.

2 Lucre Grange, near Fordingbridge. On his stay here in 1935, Berlin recorded that he tipped the butler 10/6d.

3 Samuel Ainsworth de Montmorency Drudge (1898–1970), Fellow of

Wadham College, author of *Some Little Travels in the Levant* (1932).

4 To my eternal regret and shame I have been unable to decipher the real identities behind these amusing soubriquets.

5 The Hon Robert Twistleton-Byng (1914–99), son of Lord Mulcaster, sportsman, socialite and alcoholic.

MAURICE BOWRA: A LIFE

LESLIE MITCHELL

. . . It was in the spring of 1939, with storm clouds gathering across Europe, that Maurice became involved in perhaps the most legendary episode of his disputatious Oxford career: the unusually vexed question of who should succeed Professor Horace Yaughn to the Chair of Sanskrit. The leading candidate, hotly supported by Bowra's old *bête noire*, Dame Enid Starborgling of Somerville, of whose hairstyle he is once supposed to have remarked 'All the colours of the Rimbaud', was Dr Hiram Oaks. 'But I don't at all pine for Oaks to be at the 'elm,' Bowra is reliably reported to have complained. A second aspirant, the celebrated American scholar Silas Bole of the University of New Dworkin, was also found wanting. 'On the whole, not Bole,' Bowra pronounced. Lady Primula Tanqueray is thought to have fainted with delight when this *bon mot* was conveyed to her at the breakfast table at Poshleigh Grange, Salop, where Bowra enjoyed so many stimulating weekends.

Amidst the cares of office and the internecine politicking that gave pre-war Oxford its distinctive savour, Bowra managed to find time for a relaxing holiday with his friends Reggie Simper, the brilliant young fellow of All Souls, and the Hon. Gavin Twisk. Writing from Berlin to his friend the Countess of Axminster, in one of the witty communications for which he is so renowned, he disclosed that 'it is all highly agreeable, and the Germans are all most accommodating – particularly the boys one meets in the Unter den Linden. Reggie has caught a picturesque disease and Gavin has been very naughty. Meanwhile I have been thinking hard about the heritage of symbolism. Professor D'Ulle's death, is of course, a great blow.' The irony of that last sentence would not have been lost on his correspondent . . .

. . . The first fruit of these lucubrations was Bowra's influential study *Attic Wanderings*. Its opening paragraph may be taken as the summation of everything he believed in, his insistence on truth, individual responsibility and the humanist pursuit of all that is best and good in life. 'The poet,' he wrote, 'is really rather a special chap, not at all like those ghastly bank-clerks and the politicians who go about stopping us having a good time. It is our duty to furnish the conditions in which the productions of his muse may best be realised – elegantly panelled rooms, lots of friends to gossip with and plenty of servants. But, of course, nobody really cares about art these days.'

The failure of *Attic Wanderings* and its successor, the autobiographical *Ramblings*, to win a permanent place in the literature of our time was one of Bowra's most grievous disappointments. And yet it is Maurice's influence on so many succeeding generations that remains his most lasting memorial. As Gervase Drudge, later a senior official in the Ministry of Pensions, recalled: 'Most dons just wanted you to do tedious things like get on with your work and be a credit to the college. But Maurice was different. He wanted to have you to dinner, so he could make up smutty limericks and tell you how he hated the Professor of Greek. He encouraged us all to despise convention and achieve our full potential as human beings, and I have always been grateful to him.' Lady Stultitia Blodwyn, whose *amitie amoreuse* with Maurice must surely count as one of his most bitter-sweet relationships, agreed: 'Maurice was simply frightfully amusing. It was as if we were all at the Court of Louis XIV, and not just at Oxford listening to some egotistical old don droning on . . .' [*continues for hundreds of pages*].

MY DEAR HUGH: LETTERS FROM RICHARD COBB TO HUGH TREVOR-ROPER AND OTHERS

TIM HEALD

Cobb's election to a fellowship at Balliol, Oxford, was testimony to his growing reputation as a scholar of revolutionary France. But to this genuine egalitarian the college's increasingly left-wing bent was a source of growing disquiet . . .

To Trevor-Roper, 30 May 1974

Dreadful news from Belial – would you believe, they have just appointed Dr Weevil as tutor for admissions? No more Etonian peers of the realm and witty boys from Winchester, alas. Dear me, how I shall miss them. We used to be distinctly aristocratic here, before 'progress' laid its dead hand on our shoulder. One of my first pupils was Lord Mordecai Drone – undoubtedly the stupidest man I have ever met (he thought that Runnymede was an alcoholic drink) but so charming you know, and with an absolutely unrivalled taste in port. Then there was Viscount Ditchwater, whose father subscribed so handsomely to the library fund to secure his admission and can truthfully be said to have made the Vomit Club a shining example of patrician excess. Why, it is said that after one of their dinners, at which I was not myself unwelcome, *every one* of the college staircases had to be sluiced down. It is really *tragic* that such a fine old tradition of *noblesse oblige* should perish . . . [*continues*].

. . . Meanwhile, even worse news about the election for the D'Ulle Professorship. As you know, we had hoped for Silas Todhunter, a splendid drinking man from Oriel who wrote that wonderful piece in the *Anti-Democrat* about how prudent the Chileans were to get rid of Allende – why this caused such a fuss I can't imagine – but no, the electors for some inexplicable reason have settled for Dr Keith Drudge, one of those scholarly, hard-working men interested in Tudor hegemony, or some such rubbish. If only people would realise that a professor of history's real job is to cut a *figure* and write amusing articles in the *Spectator* about things that have nothing to do with his subject, then the value of education would be more appreciated by the ingrate young.

A welcome diversion from the challenges of university life came in 1984, when he was appointed to chair the judging panel for the Booker Prize for Fiction.

To Trevor-Roper, 24 October 1984

Well, it is all over and by dint of some ingenious manoeuvring I think I may be said to have done a little negative good by keeping anything with genuine literary merit – Martin Amis, Angela Carter, Lisa de Someone or Other – off the shortlist. What a blessed relief it was to be able to give the prize to Eloise Twinch's *Loosestrife*. Incidentally, whatever the press may have reported, I was *not* drunk at the ceremony – merely a couple of bottles of the Latour '45 you and Xandra so kindly gave me at Easter – and the remark that I had never read a modern novel in my life nor wanted to was meant as a *joke* . . . [*continues for hundreds of pages*].

CAST OF CHARACTERS
The Hon. Jolyon Urquhart-Smythe Undergraduate at Christ Church Oxford, where he was Custodian of the Foot Beagles, and early pupil of Cobb's. Known for his lilac-coloured waistcoats. Drank himself to death in 1965.

Gervase Ffolkes-Crenshaw Admissions tutor at Merton College for over sixty years and famous for his dismissal of T. S. Eliot's *The Wasteland*, in a celebrated review for the *Fogey* magazine, as 'the worst gardening manual ever written'. Once admitted the entire Eton rowing VIII to read Agricultural and Forest Sciences . . . [*continues*].

HUGH TREVOR-ROPER: THE BIOGRAPHY

ADAM SISMAN

. . . 1966 began auspiciously for Trevor-Roper, with an invitation to spend the New Year with his great friend Henrietta, Lady Fawning, at Poshleigh Grange in Northumberland. Here he was delighted to encounter his old acquaintance Sir John Bigotte, in whose genealogical interests – both men claiming descent from the seventeenth century Recusant scourge, Bishop D'Ulle – he took a lively interest, and to observe the survival of such charming local customs as the Twelfth Night peasant hunt. Further pleasure was assured by the publication of his latest book of essays, *Learned Trifles*, which was cordially reviewed by several old friends in the Sunday newspapers. A momentary source of irritation surfaced in the unexpected arrival of Professor Silas Drone at dinner, but happily, by feigning deafness and taking his plate to the orangery (where he was later found playing bezique with one of the footmen) Trevor-Roper managed to avoid speaking to his distinguished academic colleague for the entire evening.

It was at this point, friends attest, that Trevor-Roper's reputation had reached its zenith. With his bow-ties, well-cut tweed suits, aristocratic wife, supercilious manner and faultless taste in claret, Oxford History had seen nothing like him. Publishers, who had courted him since his celebrated controversy with the Catholic novelist Evelyn Snargs – see the letter 'Snargs: A Witty Riposte' in the *Daily Telegraph* of 15 June 1957, reprinted in his wide-ranging collection *Some Old Book Reviews* (1963) – petitioned him by every post. In this year alone he agreed to write a comprehensive analysis of the great religious and political questions of the early modern period entitled *Why I am Absolutely Right about Everything*, as well as a searing apologia for the historian's craft called *Brooking no Dissent*. That neither book ever appeared can only be explained by the immense administrative responsibilities and punishing workload to which he was subject at this time.

Returning to Oxford, where he was forced to sit through a number of tedious dinners at his college, Oriel ('I suspect several of the fellows of not having gone to decent schools, and the cellar is not what it was,' he commented to his friend Lady Mortitia Starborgling), he immediately rejoined the academic fray with a highly amusing letter to the *New York Times Book Review*, under the pseudonym 'Laetitia Gusset', ridiculing his fellow scholar Alceste Boag. Yet a much more serious opponent was at hand. Opening the pages of the *Times Literary Supplement* he discovered an article by the young historian Keith Drudge entitled 'Fact has its place', in which Trevor-Roper's essay 'Some Frightfully Witty Remarks about Witchcraft' was criticised for alleging that Baron Stoat (1549–1617) lived in Norfolk rather than the Isle of Wight, had red hair, not black, three children not ten, and died not of syphilis but opium addiction. Trevor-Roper responded with his customary vigour, accusing Drudge of being 'a silly ass' and 'not quite a gentleman', and would, experts agree, probably have written a definitive defence of his position (the proposed book, entitled *Why I Hate Mr Drudge*, was contracted to messrs Macmillan but sadly never appeared) had he not been engaged on a series of delightful articles about Oxford *mores* for the *Spectator* – see *The Snobbe Papers* (1970) – in the guise of a fourteenth century archdeacon.

A lesser man might have quailed before these onslaughts. Trevor-Roper would undoubtedly have been consoled by the encomium pronounced by his young admirer Dr Hyacinth Fogey: 'Dear Hugh, he really was a sweetie. He had *flair*, you see, and he was really so frightfully witty. Of course, he may have got his facts wrong from time to time, and pursued all those tedious vendettas, but oh dear me such a *relief* from all the frightful bores who teach history at Oxford now . . .' [*continues for hundreds of pages*].

BIOGRAPHICAL
PORTRAITS

SOMEWHERE TOWARDS THE END

DIANA ATHILL

RELIGION

Well really, you know, if God were to exist, I think he would be rather foolish. Naturally, there would probably be people who wished to console themselves with what he had to say, but I should not be among them. Of course, the poor sillies would be perfectly entitled to do this.

SEX

I have never been able to appreciate the tremendous fuss that is made about sexual fidelity. When a man betrays his wife, or vice-versa, why can he not follow the admirable Gallic model and commit adultery *properly*? I remember that when my boyfriend Barry succumbed to the attractions of a much younger woman – darling Sally, who has since become one of my dearest friends – I at once invited her into our house, made sure that a space was available for her toothbrush at the bathroom sink, and went so far as to design the two of them matching embroidered 'his' and 'hers' pillow cases using a crochet stitch taught to me by my mother. At the time it seemed the only civilised thing to do.

THE YOUNG

To meet young people, as I am lucky enough to do from time to time, is always a very illuminating experience. Given how busy they are, with their Greek dancing lessons and their interest in Mr Lonnie Donegan's 'Skiffle' music, it is extremely kind of them to take the trouble with us old fogies, and I am grateful. But we must not expect this attention as a right. I once sat at dinner next to a lively man in his late sixties or seventies who announced that he got on very well with young people and seemed to feel that he was the same age as them. What a silly man he was!

ON LATE-FLOWERING SUCCESS

I was, of course, extremely flattered that the memoir of my early years, *Tea with Mrs Fothergill*, and the account of my time in publishing, *Dinner at André's*, should have found so many enthusiastic readers. Equally I was highly flattered to be asked to appear on the radiogram with Miss Sue Lawley. But really, you know, enjoyable as all this was, I can't think why I wrote the books at all, and would prefer them not to be mentioned . . . [*continues*].

INSTEAD OF A BOOK

DIANA ATHILL

These letters belong to my dear friend Edward Field, to whom they were written. He decided that he wanted them to be published. I have no idea why – D. A.

Darling Edward,

What an old silly you are to think that Gentlemen's Relish is a traditional American condiment! Why, my nanny used to spread it on toast for me when I was a girl. It came in the most elegant circular pots, whose top half fitted neatly into the lower, and one could have the greatest fun prising them apart with the end of a knife. My mother, I seem to remember, had her own variation on the receipt which involved substituting grilled sardines for anchovies and adding rather too much pepper . . . [*continues*]. It is fascinating to learn how much you are enjoying Hector Baugh's *Darkness at the Tunnel's End*. We published it when I was at André Deutsch, in a wonderful series that also included fine work by Quentin Teigh-Diem and Lorenzo D'Ulle, and I had high hopes for it – the scene in which Yaughn, the hero, stands skimming stones into the wild ocean is particularly engrossing – but the reviewers were such sillies and said it was incomprehensible and in the end it only sold seven copies.

We are having a splendid time here getting ready for Christmas. Barry is, I believe, going to Sally's to take advantage of her Sky television satellite apparatus, and has cooked a wonderful Jamaican chicken dish for us to eat. Meanwhile, I have a discovered a very useful thing now stocked by Safeway's. This is a loaf of bread, to all intents and purposes normally constituted, yet already cut into slices – perfect for popping into a toaster, or when one doesn't wish to eat a great deal. Do they have them in New York, I wonder?

It was terribly kind of you to offer advice about our gas-fire. Fortunately we have found an absolutely dreamy man called Eric who has promised to put in a nice little new heater whose fumes *won't* blow back in the annoying way that they usually do . . . [*continues for several pages*]. I am making good progress with my memoir, and the publishers seem pleased, though I can't imagine why anyone should be interested in such a forgetful old personage as myself. I have just reached the part where Vidia throws one of his tantrums and hides behind the sofa. Wasn't he a silly?

UNDER THE SUN: THE LETTERS OF BRUCE CHATWIN

ELIZABETH CHATWIN AND NICHOLAS SHAKESPEARE

TO BOFFLES STARBORGLING

Eremites Cell, Monastery of St Basil the Incurable, Ankara, August 1978

Dearest Bo,

I simply can't think what I'm doing confined here amid all this hideous statuary. On the other hand, I have swum the Bosphorus twice, on the second occasion attended by three Turkish princesses in a very nice *caique*, which was most refreshing. And of course, *le tout Ankara* comes to visit: Bunty and Perdita are at their castle – he is the Akond of Swat's dentist, I believe, and she a great expert on the Dahomey fruitbat – not to mention those two contessas that Willie Maugham introduced me to when we were staying with Noel that time at Cap Ferrat. But you are right, of course – the answer is to live alone.

Much love, Bruce

*Forced to leave Benin as a result of the military coup, and
what he described as the 'rather too marked attentions'
of its despot, General Fang, Chatwin immediately
departed by jet-ski and hang-glider to New York to
spend the winter with Robert Mapplethorpe, Jackie
Onassis and Henry Kissinger, with whom he planned
to collaborate in a book about the little known* bogusi
*tribe of Upper Volta. His friend Robin Kent-Cumberland
remembered this period in his life: 'Dear Jackie, it was
quite a relationship. She loved him almost as much as
he loved himself.'*

TO MRS CECILY PIGEON

Booth of the Kif-smokers, Khan-El-Khallili Bazaar,
Cairo, March 1979

Dear Mrs Pigeon,
    I was extremely sorry to receive your letter
accusing of me of secretly copying out large parts
of your father's journal *What I Did In Patagonia*
when I stayed at your house and then putting
them in my book, *Journey to Nowhere*, without your
permission. I can only state in my defence that art
sometimes moves in mysterious ways.

    Yours with deepest regret
    Bruce Chatwin

TO BEVERLEY CLEVERLEY

Somewhere in darkest Africa, June 1980

Dear Bev,

Of *course* you can borrow my flat in Albany. It is, however, the merest *garçonnière*, and my tastes, I must warn you, are deeply Spartan. In fact, apart from the Louis XVI ormolu-plated wash-hand stand, the Sheraton sofa, the Queen of Haiti's ceremonial tea-towel (framed) and that first Sanskrit edition of the *Mahabharana* that Salman Rushdie was kind enough to annotate for me, there's so very little in the way of ornament that I doubt it would be worth your while.

Love to Constancia
Bruce

In August Chatwin travelled by pony and ant-eater ('it really is extraordinarily comfortable – you use the proboscis as a kind of steering-wheel') to Quito, Ecuador to go snorkelling in Lake Poultice with his young friend Aloysius Vole-Trouser. 'There was no one like him,' Vole-Trouser recalled. 'To have a rich wife and a series of agreeable bolt-holes in far-flung parts of the world is a devastating combination.'

TO ELIZABETH CHATWIN

Third Hut, Tensing Gorge, Nepal, September 1982

This is the highest imaginable camp before the mountains proper. A few days of wind-surfing and vulture-tagging before Pope John-Paul II (very agreeable, and a great authority on the Mongolian *daktari* dialect, on which I may write a monograph) flies me off to Lake Oboe. Viking paying huge sums of money for book – apparently. Please send £1,000 by return.

Might see you next year, if I'm strapped for cash

XXX
B

Early in 1985 Patrick Leigh-Fermor wrote to the Duchess of Devonshire: 'Dearest Debo, Annoying young twit called Bruce Chatwin staying here. Knows everyone. Ever heard of him?' The Duchess replied: 'Darling Padders, Bruce Chatwin! He wrote that simply divine book about wherever it was he went to and whatever it was he did when he got there. I'm simply mauve with envy. But how twinch if he's a know-all. Should we invite him to dins, do you think . . .?' [continues for hundreds of thousands of pages].

CHARLES DICKENS: A LIFE

CLAIRE TOMALIN

. . . There is of course very little actual proof that Dickens despatched his mistress Ellen Ternan to France in the period 1862–1865, visited her on numerous occasions and had an illegitimate child by her which died, and yet the circumstantial evidence is so very strong that a biographer would be mad not to fill an entire chapter with it so the newspapers have something to serialise (*surely 'set down the known facts in an objective and responsible manner'? – Ed.*). Take, for example, a letter of September 1863 in which Dickens informs Mrs Edith Brisket, his landlady at Wellington Street, that he will have 'chops and sauce in the usual way'. In the circumstances it is hardly coincidental that 'Sauce' was the name of a lively cocker-spaniel owned by a neighbour of the Ternan family when they resided at Haywards Heath sometime in the 1850s. Similarly, when Dickens chose the name of 'Hexham' for the corpse-dredging Thames lighterman of *Our Mutual Friend* – then taking shape in his mind – he would have been all-too aware that Mrs Ternan and her daughters had very nearly visited Hexham in Northumberland on their summer holiday of 1857, only deciding to make their way to Whitby at the very last moment.

Dickens's letters of the period are, if anything, even more suggestive. There is, for instance, a note to his friend Silas Minion from 1864, in which, recounting the circumstances of a stormy cross-channel voyage, he remarks, 'We have been through hell and high water, and must turn and turn again.' The alert reader will note the private code that this consciously or sub-consciously betrays ('hell and . . .' = 'Ellen', 'turn and turn' = 'Ternan'). It is even possible to insinuate this sadly anonymous young woman into the narrative of Dickens's death. Although the scene of his passing is always assumed to be his house at Gadshill near Rochester in Kent, it is perfectly possible that he may have suffered his fatal stroke at his paramour's Peckham lodgings, and been conveyed by her – Ellen was a strong girl and quite capable of this feat – by cab, locomotive (Bradshaw reveals that a 3.17 ran from Holborn Viaduct to nearby Chatham) and penny-farthing bicycle to the family home. Alternatively, it is by no means stretching credulity to wonder whether Miss Ternan could have hired an air balloon for the purpose. As for

her proposed co-authorship of *Great Expectations,
Our Mutual Friend* and *The Mystery of Edwin Drood,*
well . . . [*continues*].

JOURNALS VOLUME I

JOHN FOWLES

3 October 1949
Life: an irregular conjunction of particularities.

10 October 1949
Oxford imponderable under her grey stones and skies. My first tutorial with Professor Dull: dry, exact, meticulous, without humour. He fails to appreciate that beneath my insouciant manner and pitiless disinclination to do any work moves a coruscating intelligence. But I shall be revenged on this pack of vulgar fools.

2 March 1951
Eventually.

6 September 1951
At home with my parents: a day of savage tragedy. Myself, mute, absorbed in Hugh Delacourt Heigh's *Highbrow Sonatas* on the Third Programme; my mother engaged in some futile domestic task. All

is arid, base, unkempt; the only real element my deracination. Yet I do not repine.

12 May 1952
Death: a candle flame suddenly extinguished, the hand unseen. The moth fluttering.

14 June 1952
Greece. I find the place agrees with me, though food, work, companions seedy and mediocre. I tolerate life. A fugitive, tatterdemalion quality that soothes. Nietzsche, Kierkegaard felt this, I believe. My book returned for the 37th time: the proud scars of rejection.

3 April 1962
Finally. My agent, a devious fellow, writes to say that I am to be given a large sum of money for my novel, *The Introvert*. It is nothing but my due, yet in any true sense the prospect appals me. Hollywood vulgarising my words, the praise of a multitude that is not worth having. I spurn them as I savour the bread they throw.

4 June 1964
Butter: more nutritious than margarine, I conclude. Yet there are some wounds that shall not heal.

SHADES OF GREENE: ONE GENERATION OF AN ENGLISH FAMILY
JEREMY LEWIS

. . . If Graham Greene (known to his cousins as 'Boffles' or occasionally 'Greeney', to the young ladies he met in the course of his perambulations along Bond Street as 'Dearie', but to his chauffeur by the more formal salutation 'Mr Greene') was by this time well-established in his trade as a novelist, the career followed by his little-known cousin Hyacinth Greene was no less fascinating. Joining the literary agency of Ditchwater & Dulle in the June, or possibly the July of 1947, first at their offices at 17 Shoreditch High Street – convenient for the tobacconist next door where he was able to purchase the Sahib Virginia Straight Cut cigarettes favoured by all members of the Greene family – but shortly afterwards removing to 137b the Mile End Road as a result of LCC building regulations – Hyacinth was very soon able to play what by all accounts was a pivotal role in the agency's post-war development, when they represented such well-known authors as Millicent Dinge, Sadie Blackeyes and the Hon. Cecil Fauntleroy, author of *Pastel Pencillings* and the immortal *Dewdrops Do Drop*.

'I don't know quite what Mr Greene did,' Miss Ethel Frobisher, who acted as secretary-typist to the firm in the winter of 1947, having formerly been charwoman to Charlie Chaplin's maternal great-aunt, remembered, 'but I'm sure he did it very well. He once asked me to go the pictures with him but it was the night I washed my hair so I had to say no.' Relations between the two cousins remained close: 'Dear Hi,' Graham wrote in the January of 1948, 'Not another blooding sponging letter! Next time you ask me for money I shan't even reply. Now, fuck off.' At the reception following Hyacinth's wedding to the mercurial Gladys Spode, daughter of the renowned variety hall comedian Norbert 'Nobby' Spode, remembered even now for his catch-phrase 'If there's a ferret up yer trousers, I'm not getting it out', held in the upstairs bar of the Dog & Partridge, Limehouse, he was discovered to have sent the present of an ormulu-plated fish-slice, purchased at Selfridges for a princely £2.4s 7d . . .

. . . Hyacinth's social life at this time filled numberless compartments. He and Gladys are once supposed to have arrived at a friend's supper-party at Claridge's only twenty-seven minutes after Winston Churchill had left it. On another occasion, A. J. P. Taylor is thought to have handed him his overcoat in a restaurant foyer, mistakenly believing him to be a waiter. Yet he seems to have had ample time to monitor the progress of his younger sister Ariadne, whose employments at this time included acting as companion to the Dowager Duchess of Moulting at her London residence, 17 Kensington High Street, and officiating as deputy caller at Monty McGruber's celebrated Bingo Palace in the Old Kent Road. Graham was at this time in Indo-China where his guilt, sexual obsessions and deep-seated ambivalence about the Catholic church continued to . . . [*continues for thousands of pages*].

RUPERT HART-DAVIS: MAN OF LETTERS

PHILIP ZIEGLER

. . . It was at this time, with the affairs of the pub-
lishing firm that bore his name lurching from one
crisis to another, that Hart-Davis began work on his
justly celebrated biography of the novelist Hugh
Massingberd Twinkie, author of *Droop*, *Dahlias* and
In My Window Box. The work was congenial to him.
As he wrote to his great friend and fellow-Etonian
(they shared the distinction of being the only two
Lower Boys ever to have been 'up' to Silas 'Corks'
McGarrigle for extra Greek five terms running) Sir
Jasper Beamish, 'I am having the most glorious time
with dear old Hugh and have really found out some
fascinating stuff, I think. Did you know, for example, that the old boy collected fabric samples, and
had a superstitious fear of beetles? And that the
woman to whom *Sad Lilacs* is dedicated was not his
cousin but his aunt by marriage? It will all make a
wonderful book when the time comes.'

Although Rupert Hart-Davis Limited published
some works of genuine merit – one might instance

Sylvester Dull's *Ezra Pound and Campanology* or Myrtle Loosestrife's sadly neglected novel *Gosh What Larks* – their proprietor's disdain for commercial solvency was, alas, to prove its undoing, and in 1956 the firm was taken over by the more sober-minded concern of Tender & Mainprice.

Something of Hart-Davis's inner disquiet at this period may be detected in the passionate letter he wrote to his long-serving secretary, Miss Eleanor Frisky, whom he later married, while she was away from the office recovering from toothache: 'The MCC prospects are, as you say, fairly encouraging, and if Compton can only keep his place he may inject some backbone into what has hitherto been a jolly flabby lot. These Tender & Mainprice chaps are the limit, by the way. Always moaning about money, which, as you know, I simply can't be got to care about. And then at the board luncheon the chairman absolutely ate his asparagus with a fork!'

As might be expected from such a versatile editor, biographer, reviewer and compiler, the extent of Hart-Davis's literary knowledge was formidable. Notwithstanding a natural courtesy, his opinions were always vigorously expressed. He considered *Ulysses*, for example, to be 'jolly rot' and Samuel Beckett to be 'an absolute rotter'. Pride of place in this demonology was reserved for *The Wasteland*. 'Quite the worst gardening book I've ever come across,' he complained to Beamish. 'Lots of jolly good stuff at the start about watering your roots with spring rain but after that I simply couldn't make head or tail of it.'

Retiring to the North Yorkshire dales in the mid-1960s, he received news of the conferral of a knighthood. 'Dear Rupert,' his friend 'Boffles' Abercrombie, who had the ear of the court, enquired. 'Do you fancy a gong? Just say the word and I'll wangle it with HM.' Immensely proud of this decoration, which he rightly adjudged a tribute to his years of unstinting service to the publishing industry, Hart-Davis enjoyed a long and productive retirement, editing the letters of the little-known Victorian *rondelier* poet Esme Dymme, and compiling an eight-volume collection of . . .

EDWARD HEATH:
THE AUTHORISED
BIOGRAPHY
PHILIP ZIEGLER

Edward Heath was a very remarkable man. Though comparatively humbly born and blessed with a by no means outstanding intellect, he nevertheless managed to get himself elected to the House of Commons, rose to the position of Prime Minister, and remained a prominent political personality for nearly half a century. These achievements did him the greatest credit, and serve to remind us what a truly remarkable man he was.

Yet wholly admirable as were Heath's attributes, his sense of inner conviction, his well-nigh indomitable drive and his unsparing attention to detail, the less appetising – if not downright unsavoury – aspects of his character should not be ignored by the scrupulous biographer. He was, for example, fat, pompous, overbearing, mean, rude, snobbish, tufthunting, discourteous . . . [*continues*]. None of this, of course, has the slightest bearing on what a truly remarkable man he was and how greatly we should value his contribution to the life of our age.

At the same time, it would foolish to deny that, during his long career in the upper echelons of the Conservative Party, Heath had his detractors. Sir Tufton Snargs, who worked with him in the Whips' Office from March to April 1953, complained that he was 'an absolute little counter-jumping rotter'. Snargs' hostility may, of course, be only that of the distinguished country gentleman rightfully affronted by the less polished manners of the careerist grammar school-boy. More convincing, perhaps, is the testimony of Jolyon Rhodes-Beamish MP, who recalled Heath remarking to him, as they contemplated the solitary remaining dessert on a House of Commons canteen trolley, 'If you take that chocolate éclair, Rhodes-Beamish, I'll see you never sit on the 1922 Backbench Committee again.'

To set against these criticisms, which I regret to say are by no means isolated instances of Heath's ability to annoy, enrage and alienate his political allies . . . [continues for several pages] comes this warm and unsolicited tribute from his cleaning lady, Mrs Ethel Gherkin, who observed that 'Mr Heath was probably quite a nice sort of person when you got to know him.' None of this, as I have said before, in the least detracts from what a very remarkable man Heath was and what a pleasure it has been to write this book about him.

On the other hand, only the most slavish hagiographer could fail to draw attention to Heath's almost calamitous lack of political judgment, his conspicuous failure to win the General Election of February 1974, his undignified efforts to hang onto power after he lost, his altogether ludicrous attempt to retain the leadership of the Conservative Party after losing a second General Election eight months later, and the twenty-year sulk in which he took refuge after Mrs Thatcher's succession. Neither, alas, can he ignore the fact that the books on which much of Heath's later celebrity rested – *Snaps from My Holiday Album, Gleanings from My Wastepaper Basket* and other works – were merely pot-boiling trifles, or that many of the political interventions of the 1980s and 1990s were designed only to embarrass those in positions of power from which he believed he had (no doubt unfairly) been excluded.

In conclusion, I should like to say what a truly remarkable man Heath was and how much I have enjoyed the years spent in his company. It was very kind of Lord Armstrong to allow me to write the book and even kinder of him to puff it on the jacket. From what I know of Heath's character – which, alas, duty requires me to observe was self-obsessed to the point of monomania – I imagine he would not have approved of it, but I hope that he would have agreed that I have tried to do my very best on his behalf.

LETTERS TO MONICA

PHILIP LARKIN: Edited by Anthony Thwaite

27 APRIL 1955

11 Outlands Road, Cottingham, E. Yorks

Darlingest of Buns,

I hope and trust that your burrow remained sandy and dry after I had left, that Mrs Flopsy Bunny made you a sustaining mug of camomile tea and there were no depredations by Mr McGregor . . . [*continues*]. But oh dear, the rest of the weekend put me in a considerable fluster. You see, I had to buy my copy of the *Observer* – was my poem in this week? I wot not, the fuckers* – from a different shop, as the one I normally go to was closed, and oh, the mean and altogether sinister *frightfulness* of it, the yawning counter, the newsagent glaring at me and asking, 'What did I want?' Just read Orwell's *Nineteen Eighty-Four* again, and of course it's *exactly* like round here.

But here's your poem, darling, as promised:

> Sodding Vice-Chancellors, don't you just hate 'em?
> Children on fairy cycles – why not sedate 'em?
> Send home the niggers, string up the reds
> And let us librarians sleep safe in our beds

Five minutes later – No, I can't do anything at all – it is really is *appalling*. That woman below actually *whistling as she comes up the stairs*! And the noise, like a kind of endlessly churning *Niagara* filling the whole house with its wretched disturbance. The whole family blatantly *talking at meal-times* when they know I'm sitting here trying to listen to 'Hot' Pee-Wee Cystitis and his Cisco Six. Can my life get any worse? Can it? Quarter to eleven. The clock staring at me with its face of awful reproach. Just read John Wain's new one. No good, of course. And to make matter worse a telephone call from those vile, awful, unspeakable, conniving fools in Loughborough** asking if I want to come for Christmas . . .

Later still . . . But I haven't, dearest bun – did I say that I have saved a carrot for you? A nice big orange one – we can eat it together (*drawing of rabbits frolicking*) – replied to your letter.*** Please don't be miserable about all this. I shall be glad to have your sympathy, but I think we both feel that the best thing at present is that I shag my secretary and that other woman Monday to Fridays but come and see you at the weekends. Oh, how unutterably unsatisfactory life is.

Even later . . . Really pissed now, I'm afraid. That South African cooking sherry again. Good stuff but *7/9d the bottle*, would you believe it? Just been reading Yeats. No good of course. And then K's novel.**** Funny opening scene naturally taken from that phone conversation we had in January 1947. And then the joke about the woman burning the gravy from a letter I wrote to him in August 1951. I mean, it stands to reason that K. couldn't write something like that without my help. Dialogue on p. 94 with its repetition of 'breakfast' and 'cigarette-lighter', both words frequently used by me. I ask you!

Just been browsing through Enright's new collection (one of my 'contemporaries'.) No good, of course.

Good night, my hutch-trained, gentle-eyed, lettuce-loving bun.

PX

---

*L's poem, 'Staring miserably out of the window, again' appeared in the *Observer* of 4 May 1955

**L's sister and brother-in-law

***In a letter of 19 April Monica had written that she was 'desperately miserable', feared that L would never marry her and was 'distraught' over his affairs with other women

****Kingsley Amis's novel, *Friends and Other Enemies* (1955)

ROSAMOND LEHMANN

SELINA HASTINGS

. . . As spring gave way to summer there were more opportunities to spend time away from Poshleigh Grange. Not only were there delicious days in Suffolk – stalking poor people through the ancestral heather, riding on gun-limbers dragged by obsequious gamekeepers – but also weekends at Lucre Terrace, idling, sleeping and counting money. Recently their friends the Runcible-Spoones had bought Scotland, a splendidly isolated fastness somewhere north of Hadrian's Wall, for the fishing and snipe-shooting. 'Scotland is rather a marvellous place – quite too too unreal with its picturesque inhabitants, its divine rocks and heather and its nutritious porridge,' Rosamond wrote with her characteristic enthusiasm for unfamiliar milieux.

In spite of these pleasant distractions, however, Rosamond was privately determined that she would not, could not, remain in Newcastle, whose smell she had come finally to distrust. She tried to persuade Leslie to buy Hampshire, but he refused to consider it. Meanwhile, her relationship with the Hon. Wogan Twytte had reached such a pitch that their great family friend, the Marchioness of Tarradiddle, was disposed to exercise her legendary wit by remarking 'Twytte to woo?' Wogan, passionate, excitable, dim, and the owner of several well-cut evening suits, was already noted, even in the social exalted circles in which he moved (his eyebrows had excited the admiration of Lytton Strachey), for his remarkable charisma. 'At Oxford I was mad, wild, drunk with freedom, sent mad with success and down for good,' he recalled . . .

It was this time – extraordinarily considering the emotional pressures to which she was subject – that Rosamond's first novel, *Isn't This Frightfully Good?* was despatched to Chatto & Windus. 'Crikey what a stunner,' the firm's chief editor, Mr Harold Snargs, is thought to have remarked. 'Great distinction and enormous pulling power. In addition we greatly admire the book.' Nevertheless, the summer found Rosamond . . . [*continues for hundreds of pages*].

GRUB STREET IRREGULAR: SCENES FROM LITERARY LIFE

JEREMY LEWIS

I was a hopeless child: dim, backward, craven, retiring, self-conscious, devoid of all artistic or literary talent, incontinent, tone-deaf, speechless and inept. Not much has changed. From an early age I knew that finding paid employment would be tricky in the light of these disabilities. But if St Cake's, where I spent my formative years, prepares you for one thing it's finding the job for which you are suited, and so I ended up in publishing.

Sitting one day in my office at Overprint and Remainder, while recovering from the statutory five-hour lunch – these were more expansive days before the accountants and their wretched economies prevailed – I looked up to find the figure of Lt Colonel 'Bunty' Deepleigh-D'Ulle advancing upon me. Dressed in a dark herringbone overcoat, heather-mixture cavalry twill trousers, a lovat tweed sports jacket with a somewhat loud orange overcheck, spats, grey Oxfords and a knotted foulard scarf in a shade somewhere between cerulean and cornflower blue whose colour contrasted oddly with the iris of his glass eye . . . [*continues for several paragraphs*] he was carrying a copy of his travel book *The Little I Saw of Cuba*, which I had always greatly admired.

This was the beginning of a long and cordial friendship, although, nervous and tongue-tied as I was, I could never think of anything to say to him, while he, as befitted a man who had once cut off a Yugoslav partisan's head with a tin-opener, usually preferred to communicate by carrier pigeon. For some reason his *With Rod and Gun Through Roxburghshire* sold only eleven copies, six of them to the author himself at discount, but I was immensely proud to have published it.

Another friend from this time was Barbara Baugh, widow of the celebrated critic Hugh Carnapathy Hee, whose autobiography *Some Chaps I Knew* I remembered liking at prep school. Not that our relationship wasn't without its ups and downs. Barbara, who had also been married to Lord Crasher and Desmond Entirely-Forgotten, whose memoirs *Droop, Dahlias!* and *In My Window Box* I had greatly admired, had a volatile temperament. 'Jeremy,' she would say, 'you're fucking useless. Why do you always bring Moët when you know I only drink Bollinger? And what's the point of having deferential unpaid help when its fucking car won't start?' What a grand girl she was and how I appreciated her subtle sense of humour. The red mark on my forehead, legacy of the time she hurled an ashtray previously owned by her seventh husband the French poet Jean-Marie Ennui, author of *Les Mouers Atroces*, which I greatly admired, is perhaps the proudest scar I bear.

Having said goodbye to publishing, I embarked happily on a freelance career, writing reviews for *Yawn*, *Witter*, the *Weekly Somnambulist* and other papers too numerous to mention. Knowing something of my tastes and inclinations, Richard Ingrams was kind enough to offer me a job on the *Oldie*, where I . . . [*continues for hundreds of pages*].

SUPERMAC: THE LIFE OF HAROLD MACMILLAN

D. R. THORPE

... The other dispositions, in this most tantalising of reshuffles, were more straightforward. Sir Reginald Weems (of whom Macmillan remarked, 'Nice little chap with the rather common wife, looks like one of my grouse-beaters') continued as Under-Secretary in the Department of Tape & Sealing Wax, while the disputatious Hon. Hyacinth Frobisher, a much-underestimated figure (and incidentally Captain of Gremlins during Macmillan's time at Eton) whose later support for Sir Cyril Hopbine at the Foreign Office in the course of the now somewhat forgotten Ugandan affair, was unhappily to call his loyalty into question, moved, not wholly amenably, to Agriculture & Fisheries ... [*continues*].

Alas, one formerly trusted subordinate whose reckless behaviour in government – in particular the memorable occasion on which he, perhaps deliberately, omitted to wear his Old Etonian tie at dinner – could no longer be tolerated was Sir Anstruther Vole, the increasingly erratic member for Loamshire Central. Their conversation at this moment of crisis is worth recording in full. 'I say, Vole,' Macmillan remarked, as they met on the steps of Number Ten on their way to the Eton–Harrow match at Lords, 'I've been thinking about it a great deal, and we really can't have this kind of behaviour any more, you know.' 'I say, can we not?' Vole is thought to have replied. 'Dash it, have I been a frightful twit again?' 'I'm afraid so, old man,' Macmillan informed him, with the steely suavity that was his trademark, 'but give my regards to Lady Mortitia, won't you?'

And yet, it cannot be too firmly stressed, politics to Macmillan were by no means the whole of life. Waiting for his constituency result to be declared at the General Election of 1959 ('rather an oik' he noted of his Labour opponent, Gerald Kaufperson, 'and a bit Jewish-looking') he could be found reading his beloved *Pride and Prejudice* ('really frightfully good') and *Oliver Twist* ('quite excellent, and very Dickensian'). His interest in the publishing firm that bore his name continued to bear fruit, and his determined championing of the novelist Muriel Snargs did much to maintain the company's reputation. 'Dear Miss Snargs,' he wrote in 1963, with the easy wit and perceptive geniality that distinguished his correspondence, 'your new novel is frightfully brilliant and I enjoyed it enormously.'

. . . My own first encounter with this distinguished figure came in 1975 when I visited him in retirement at Birch Grove. A single log burned fitfully in the grate: to hand on a nearby table lay the newly published biography of his old political associate, Sir Oswald Looney. 'My dear fellow, do come in,' he remarked, when he met me at the door, 'you'll find the boiler in the little room at the foot of the stairs.' Happily, once this mistake had been cleared up, he entertained me with the most fascinating reminiscences of Sir Jolyon Gore-Urquhart, assistant chief whip during the reign of the legendary 'Boffles' Hardwick (1952–53) with whom, as a schoolboy, Macmillan had enjoyed many a game of Eton Fives. 'Here young man,' he said, pressing something into my hand as I got up to leave, 'I should like you to have this.' No ten-shilling note was more cherished, and I have it still . . . [*continues for thousands of pages*].

MARIE ANTOINETTE

ANTONIA FRASER

The new year of 1776 produced climactic conditions of unprecedented severity. Mist rose. Fog enveloped. Snow fell. Ancient sledges, their harnesses sedulously polished, their runners gleamingly refurbished, were prettily sent forth to bowl once more over the roads near Versailles. Yet ensconced in her sylvan bower, solitary, detached from both maternal caresses and husbandly affection, Marie Antoinette knew that in her heart there burned an unquenchable flame. The flame of Venus.

This flame did not, however, resemble the amorous conflagrations so wantonly stoked by less discreet members of the royal entourage, those bold females of whom the memorialist Baron d'Armagnac remarked, 'levity distinguished their affiliations as brevity distinguished their wit.' The Comte de Frou-frou, a venerable thirteenth lord of the powder closet and hereditary bearer of the rouge pot, was typical of the kind of older man who appealed to the young Queen as an amusing companion. Such, in fact, was his reputation as a raconteur that Marie Antoinette is said by an anonymous frequenter of the *Jardin Anglais* to have listened enraptured to his account of having slain a peasant whose singularly odiferous nature had offended his olfactory senses . . .

It is, of course, a grotesque misrepresentation, a mere tatter's garnish, to suggest that Marie Antoinette, news of the indigency of the populace having reached her royal ear, should unthinkingly have proposed that her multitudinous subjects should, as the historical primers of a later century had it, 'eat cake'. Whatever comestibles she may have thought appropriate for satisfying the culinary requirements of her people – whether grouse, caviar or *pâté de foie gras* – it can be confidently asserted that 'cake' was not among them.

It was at this point that her eye, ever restless in its sequestration, fell upon the Duc de Doremi, whose shapely calves had long excited the ladies of the royal bedchamber. In fact, it was in this elegantly furnished rendezvous on the morning of 17th December that . . . [*continues for a further 500 pages*].

THE SECRET LIVES OF SOMERSET MAUGHAM
SELINA HASTINGS

... But it was in 1938, as storm-clouds gathered over Europe, that life at the Villa Mauresque, Maugham's sumptuous Riviera hideaway, reached a zenith of *luxe, volupté et sodomé*. With its nine acres of annually renewed lawns, manicured each morning by a platoon of scissor-wielding houseboys, its regiment of Nubian bodyguards, its immaculately accoutred yacht the *Epicene* moored in the adjoining bay, and its pack of timber wolves ready to be unleashed on poor people who rang the bell in search of fragments of discarded *pâté de foie gras*, the villa was a magnet for Maugham's galaxy of stylish and well-connected friends.

As Lady Bobo d'Armagnac, a fixture at 'Morrers' during this time, recalled in her delicate memoir *Still Waits the Cab*, 'Willie was really the most divine host, for whom nothing was too much trouble. I particularly remember the family of rare Peruvian guinea-pigs that he'd had sent over from Fortnums and trained to balance cocktail-glasses on their noses, so that they could carry very dry mint-flavoured martinis out to the guests as they sat on the terrace. Really, you know, he put the art into smart, and it's something he's never been given credit for.'

Although leaving the day-to-day running of the establishment to his attentive secretary Gavin Mincing, who as Lady Bobo recalled in her stately way, 'was always about his person', Maugham was always prepared to treat those staying at the villa to shafts of his legendary wit. When the celebrated actress Tabitha Fishcake, star of *Don't, Darling, Don't*, remarked of her recent trip to Spain that it had rained incessantly, Maugham took only a moment to remark, 'Mainly on the plain, I imagine', to the great amusement of Charlie Chaplin and the Duke of Windsor, who sat nearby.

On another occasion the distinguished physicist Sir Horace Faulks committed the unpardonable solecism of arriving at the gate without an appointment. Barely looking up from the game of Snap on which he was engaged with Douglas Fairbanks Jr, Greta Garbo and the Mahatma Gandhi, Maugham instructed his butler to 'tell Sir Horace that I am not at Ohm', a sally which caused the Mahatma to laugh so uproariously that his false teeth fell out into the *brie en gelée* which even that notorious ascetic had been prevailed upon to sample.

As an enthusiastic sponsor of his friends' careers, Maugham was always keen to entertain young men of wit, charm and vivacity of whom, as he put it, 'something might be made'. Visitors at this time included the Hon. Peregrine Joyboy, author of *Droop, Dahlias* and *Lost Amidst Loosestrife*, Hyacinth 'Frisky' Frisk, of whom Maugham observed enigmatically 'Hyacinth will undoubtedly go far on those legs of his', and the rising young interior decorator Antoine de Frou-frou. In his somewhat catty memoir, *Payment Deferred*, the Hon. Peregrine recalled that he 'only had to look at my collection of Cartier cigarette cases to remember just how much I owe to Willie'.

It is also interesting to note that Maugham wrote a great many highly successful stage plays, several of which were turned into Hollywood films, and a number of best-selling novels, which for some reason hardly anyone reads these days . . . [*continues for hundreds of pages*].

THE MITFORDS: LETTERS BETWEEN SIX SISTERS
CHARLOTTE MOSLEY

NANCY TO DIANA, 4 JULY 1925

Having a frabjous time down at Swinners*. Fruity and Wog** are here and everything is simply too killing, darling. There was a bit of an awkward moment when Farve shot a gamekeeper – you know how 'pushing' the working classes are becoming these days – but happily Ye Ancient Retainer was just divine about it and said he was proud to have his blood (of which there was rather a lot – don't get squeamish, Nard) shed by a gentleman, so that was all right.

Much love always, darling, Naunce

*Their country house at Swinbrook, Gloucestershire
**Possibly Sir Wogan Cavendish-Dilke-Fortescue (1873–1945), landowner and drunk

UNITY TO JESSICA, 1 APRIL 1936

Dearest Corpse-Chafer,

Berlin is awfully splendid. The Badger* has found me this jolly flat, previously tenanted by some Jewish people who had the misfortune to fall under a train. Too gamboge** of him, I thought. Do tell Debo that the lamp-shades are made out of real human skin, which must have cost a fortune. Goebbels, whom I don't think you've met, has been too sweet and comes round every evening to play Canasta.

Must go now darling as I have bayonet practice at 6.

Ever your loving Bobo

*Hitler
**From Krapisch, the Mitford private language, meaning "good-natured"

DEBORAH TO DIANA, 19 MAY 1942

Darling Nardy,

Thanks frightfully for the Heavener hankers* – the lady who blows my nose for me was simply *prostrate*. I forgive you being a Fascist for that.

Hope prison isn't too awful darling. Everybody is being terribly grim about you being a traitor, but I tell them all not to be so beastly to my poor Nard.

Best love, Debo.

*Apparently the gift of a set of matching handkerchiefs

JESSICA TO PAMELA, 13 JANUARY 1958

Look here Woo,

It is simply too vile and *foul* of you to suggest that I stole Muv's photo album in order to illustrate that *Life* magazine article 'Why Two of My Sisters Were Nazi Loonies' and you must consider us on non-speakers herewith.

Decca

DIANA TO DEBORAH, 25 FEBRUARY 1988

Darling Debo,

Such a beastly review of the Betj book in the *Sunday Times* by that ghastly little man Carey, saying he was vindictive, snobbish and disloyal. A nobler, funnier man never lived. Could anyone honestly believe that when he wrote that poem about 'The working classes smell/I'm sure they'll go to hell' he wasn't making a joke? The more wonderful you are the more you are resented, it seems to me.

Had a delightfully understanding phone call from Andrew [Wilson] which was too good of him. Agreed with me that he couldn't see why everyone was still so interested in us. Just a set of poor, country girls, growing up in the middle of nowhere with Muv and Farve and no money to speak, never knowing what would become of us,

not in the least interested in publicity or grand
events, but simply *hounded* by the newspapers . . .
[*continues for hundreds of pages*].

COLD CREAM: MY EARLY LIFE AND OTHER MISTAKES
FERDINAND MOUNT

It is an odd, sequestered childhood I live here in the cottage beneath the Wiltshire downs, seeing no one, preserving my embarrassed modesty with days of brooding silence, indulged only by my grandmother's nanny Miss Fothergill, who will later go on to look after David Cameron and marry the Duke of Northumberland.

'What a quiet life this is,' I remember saying to Siegfried Sassoon, or perhaps it was T. S. Eliot – I can't remember – at about this time. 'Oh, I don't know,' Sassoon remarks – in fact, now I remember, it was Eliot – 'Let's ask Graham and Evelyn here what they think.' But what Graham Greene and Evelyn Waugh think is lost in an invitation from a tall man with a moustache, who may have been Harold Macmillan, to come and play horsey-horsey on the lawn.

Although I never think to complain about it, it is a queer hand that fate has dealt me. Of course I am completely useless at everything: shy, diffident, lonely, intellectually uncertain, an eternal victim of self-doubt and the *mauvais quart d'heure*. We have no money and my father is an amateur jockey. 'If I believed for one moment in discussing affairs of a personal nature,' I tell my friend Prince Michael of Kent, when we meet at our exclusive prep school, 'I should be jolly miffed about all these terrible handicaps.' Sometimes I wonder how, in the face of these disadvantages, I manage to win a scholarship to Eton, write several well-regarded novels and edit the *Times Literary Supplement*. It can only be down to luck.

I am sixteen, gauche, spotty, inexperienced, dumb . . . [*continues*], standing with my mother before the Leaning Tower of Pisa. 'I say,' she says, staring shrewdly at the crowd of tourists. 'I'm sure I know that chap. Isn't it the Pope?' 'No,' I venture, a dim memory of one of the guests at my uncle Tony the famous novelist's house rising in my consciousness. 'Surely it's Charlie Chaplin.' 'Don't be silly,' she says. 'It's Oofy Ffiennes-Twistleton.' And so she explains about Oofy Ffiennes-Twistleton, whose real name is apparently Canteloupe-Castleton, and whose mother was Amanda Fyfe-Farthingale (née Parakeet), Viscount Voletrouser's step-daughter, and the time passes very pleasantly.

* * *

I have no idea why I am asked to work for Mrs Thatcher, as I have no real political convictions and cannot write for toffee, but somehow here I am pouring her tea in 10 Downing Street and trying to look enthusiastic. 'That's a very bad cold you have there, Ferdy,' Mrs Thatcher says.

'It's really nothing, Prime Minister,' I tell her. 'There are some aspirins in my bag,' she goes on. In my haste not to draw further attention to myself I accidentally dislodge several vases of cut flowers over her skirt and set off the fire alarm. Fortunately Mrs Thatcher is jolly decent about this, and we settle down to discuss the Falklands War.

FRANCES PARTRIDGE: THE BIOGRAPHY

ANNE CHISOLM

... The advent of the Second World War would offer the sternest test of the values that Bloomsbury held dear. Almost immediately the first of many crises presented itself when Ethel Furbelow (*'Mademoiselle fourrure-dessous'* as Frances and Ralph amusingly nick-named her) the maid-of-all-work at their agreeable Wiltshire residence Wiseacre Cottage gave notice of her intention to leave their employ for a munitions factory on the very day that Frances was due to read a paper to Bloomsbury's prestigious Trifle Club on the hitherto unexplored subject of Lytton Strachey's maternal great-aunt.

Quietly furious ('The silly woman should remember that her first duty is to civilising principles and not to making aeroplanes in which a lot of bestial young men can fly around killing each other, rot them') Frances resolved to make the tea and hand round the Bath Oliver biscuits herself. The evening, she recorded in her diary, was a triumph ('The sight of Venetia's sweet pale face under the shadow of the rhododendrons as we discussed whether Lytton's sleeping with Bobo was actually a betrayal of Constantia or an humane act of reconciliation brought home to me all the things that it is important not to fight for. I felt that I had made a small, yet infinitely important point') although she notes that she was 'terribly shaken' by Lady Stultitia Blodwyn's contention that 'battle dress is really rather fetching'.

Was all that Bloomsbury stood for to be carelessly flung into jeopardy? Frances was honest enough to admit that the behaviour of certain of their friends deeply shocked her. When the young balletomane Cyril Simper decided to enlist in the Sadler's Wells Rifles (remarking that he would 'list for a lancer, for who will sleep with the brave?') she was roused to fury ('it is simply a self-pleasing gesture, what Virginia in her devastating way would call the bath of least resistance'). What was needed, she believed, as the Panzers swept west over the Maginot Line, was rational discussion and mutual acceptance of opposing points of view. The arrest and internment of the Fifth Columnists Sir Hugo Jackboot and his wife Lady Fruitella, with whom they had enjoyed so many summer picnics on the lawn at Rantingdon, brought her no comfort ('It is simple barbarism. If Hugs and Fruity want Germany to win, why shouldn't they be allowed to say so, I wonder?').

Neither did public disquiet over Lord Howler's inflammatory broadcasts on Berlin Radio ('I can't say I like the man, but he is undoubtedly sincere in what he believes. Of course, the asses can't see that'). Sometimes the war seemed painfully close, as on the occasion when a soldier from a platoon passing through the village knocked at the door and asked if she could spare a tea-bag. 'Frankly the sight of his silly, red, pert and somehow condescending face made me feel quite sick. I wished Ralph had been there to impress upon him the consequences of his folly, but alas he was on the telephone to his stockbroker.'

But Bloomsbury, for all the strains imposed on its way of life and its traditional recreations, was still Bloomsbury. In a landscape of Stygian darkness, some beacons still shone hesitantly through the murk. The decision of the distinguished novelist Milo Camp, author of *Dadie, I Hardly Knew You* and *Dividend Payment*, to leave his wife's death-bed for the solace of the much younger Sadie Dinge brought a certain amount of soul-searching ('We decided that it was important Milo should feel himself valued at this difficult time, that there was no point in criticising a state of affairs of which we were ignorant, and of course everyone knows what Milo is like'). In December 1941 ('The Americans have entered the war – of course this is simply frightful') she was able to record that she and Ralph had discussed Freudian analyses of dreams ('He maintained that a forest, of course, represented pubic hair; I said what if it were just a forest?') and written a very interesting article for the *New Statesman*. 'It seems to me that if we can preserve one civilised outpost amid the reek and decay of our civilisation, then we shall have been true to ourselves in a way with which Lytton and Virginia would readily have sympathised . . . [*continues for a very long time*].

JOURNAL
ANTHONY POWELL

MARCH 2000

Tuesday 28 March

Woke up to find myself dead, on reflection a not wholly disagreeable state. In fact a certain status conferred: Shakespeare, Kipling, Stendhal, others one could think of, all passed through what must be admitted a disconcerting process. Absence of 'essentials of life' – *Debrett*, *Daily Telegraph*, etc. – obvious drawback, tho' not, one suspects, insuperable.

Wednesday 29 March

Arrival in Heaven. Rather a business. A great crowd of supplicants, none of them known to me, finally disposed into some kind of order by arrival of imposing figure in flowing blue and white robes (the Hon. G. H. Lyttelton's house colours). This I took to be Archangel Gabriel, tho' no formal introduction. Elysian fields, glimpsed beyond gates, not unlike lower meadows at Eton. General impression – soaring pediments, arches etc. – not at all unfavourable in point of view of architectural style, tho' could have done without interminable piped 'sacred' music.

Thursday 30 March

Dinner for new arrivals. All perfectly tolerable. God – venerable figure, curiously like Andrew (Devonshire) – perfectly all right once one gets to know him, at pains to put guests at their ease with jokes about 'fiery furnaces beneath' etc. Wine Ambrosia 2000 (I did not see the label). Conversation about war, pestilence, death etc. – not subjects on which I am outstandingly hot – but was pleased to discover that attendant cherubim distant connexion of my mother's Lincolnshire Cherry-Bymme offshoots.

Friday 31 March

Irritated to find among accounts of other new arrivals in social column of *Daily Heavenograph* reference to 'Lady Barbara Twytte' (widow of my Balliol contemporary Gavin Twytte). In fact, as merest glance at appropriate reference books could have shown – tho' possibly not procurable here – Barbara, as baronet's relict, merely 'Lady Twytte'. Naturally such sloppiness endemic 'down below', as I shall no doubt have to get used to calling it, but somewhat shocked to find celestial standards similarly lax.

HEAVEN JOURNAL

ANTHONY POWELL

21 April 2001

Somewhat surprised – as one receives few invitations these days – to be sent letter requesting attendance at Eton conference. Subject for discussion apparently oneself. Tho' long past the age at which one could be expected to derive any satisfaction from such gatherings, decided that it might be thought bad form to decline.

22 April 2001

Pre-conference luncheon at Ritz. Great crowd of persons, many of them quite unknown to me. Food – pâté de foie gras, smoked salmon, entrecôte etc. – eatable without being notably exciting. Later caught a few moments of post-luncheon address on 'The Genius of Anthony Powell'. This I was interested to hear, if conscious that certain aspects of an admittedly large subject had not been adequately dealt with. But I would hesitate to pronounce a judgement.

23 April 2001

To Eton. Here a somewhat seedy crowd had assembled: fans, academics, sprinkling of literary types, etc. Nevertheless, one felt their objectives deserving of encouragement. Glance at conference 'programme' – 'Widmerpool – our greatest comic character', 'The Achievement of Anthony Powell' and so forth, certainly subjects not without all intrinsic interest, confirmed this impression. Lunch taken in dining hall – chicken, rice, peas. To drink: tap water 2001 (I did not see the label).

24 April 2001

Various characters met on previous day (Massingberd, A. N. Wilson, etc.) given space in newspapers to reflect on proceedings at length.

ANTHONY POWELL:
A LIFE
MICHAEL BARBER

. . . It was at this point, with his magnum opus
complete, that Powell began work on his four-
volume sequence of memoirs, *To Keep the Pot Boiling*.
As he came to complete the second instalment,
Some Frightfully Amusing People One Has Known (the
opening volume, *Eton Ramblings*, had been described
by Hugh Massingberd in the *Daily Telegraph* as 'the
most agreeable portrait of C. M. Frobisher's house
yet committed to paper') he was interrupted by
controversy when the *Times* printed a letter from
the Hon Algernon Dymme, with whom Powell had
messed at Eton, alleging that his fictional anti-hero,
Kenneth Widdington, was modelled on Lord Dull,
Minister of Fisheries in the Attlee government.
Powell's response to these accusations showed him
at his most Delphic. 'The most frightfully tedious
thing about these dreadful bores who come to see
me,' he remarked, 'is that they all sort of assume
that one simply puts into the books all the people
that one knows. And if you take the trouble to

investigate, which of course scarcely anyone does these days, you'll find that Lord Dull, unlike Widdington, is actually left-handed and married to a Marquis's daughter rather than an Earl's divorced wife . . .'

. . . It was at this time that I persuaded Powell to grant me an interview at his agreeable Somersetshire residence. The entry in his *Journals* describing this encounter strikes a characteristic note: 'Really frightful character called Barber came to talk to me for some publication of which I did not catch the name. Spent the rest of the afternoon reading *Debrett*, subsequently being joined at tea by Sylvia Farquahar-Fitzlightly (nee Kent-Cumberland/Ashkenazy/Twistleton-Trevelyan), V's cousin through her Delacourt-Delingpole connection, tho' *Debrett* untypically ambiguous on this point . . .' [*continues*].

RENEGADE:
THE LIVES AND TALES OF
MARK E. SMITH
MARK E. SMITH

ON HIS EARLY LIFE

Is this fookin' thing switched on . . .? Right, then
. . . Cheers . . . No, ah'm not raising me voice,
else I'll miss the Karaoke . . . Cheers mate . . . Me
childhood? It was all right, torturing me sisters and
trading porn mags with them Irish lads. I feel sorry
for kids these days. They're missing out on things.
Not that I enjoyed myself, mind. At school they
read us the fookin' *Hobbit*. Can you imagine that?
This book about some tiny fucker who lives in a
hole. I couldn't get me head round that . . .

I couldn't afford to go to college: went for about
three months, but I never had any money. Not
that I liked it, mind, fuckers telling you what to do.
Educate yourself, that's always been my philosophy.
George V. Higgins – that's a good writer. You don't
get fellows like that on any of the reading lists.
Not, that I agree with reading lists, mind. You don't
fookin' tell me what to read . . . [*continues*].

ON HIS PUBLIC IMAGE

I really do think there's people who think I'm an aggressive character, y'know, some kind of maniac. . . Look, just fuck *off* will y'pal, else I'll . . . Right, I fookin' *told you*, you fucker . . . Anyway, it's mostly journalists as do that, that fookin' Paul Morley . . . [*rambles uncertainly for some minutes*]. Ask anyone that's been in The Fall – that bloke there, he played bass for us for ten minutes in 1980, or was it 1981 – and they'll tell y', Mark, he looks after his own. That time I clobbered Eric Lard [Fall lead guitarist, 13 September–3 October 1982] with his Fender Stratocaster – fookin' poncey guitar, I mean why couldn't he have a Woolworth's one like everyone else? – it were all over the papers – trust that fookin' Paul Morley – but what no one ever remembers is that it was me that took him down Casualty and phoned his dad to say, 'Your wanker of a son's had an accident.' Credit where credit's due. The fucker.

ON THE BAND'S EARLY DAYS

Rat Street, Prestwich was quite a going place at the time. Always plenty of vomit on the doorsteps at Christmas, which is a sign that folk aren't feeling the pinch . . . Good solid working class people . . . Not that I liked it, mind. Then when I saw the Pistols at the Lesser Free Trade Hall in '76, I thought, 'My lot aren't as bad as that.' Not that they were any good, mind. There's people who'll say, 'that Mark, he's a fookin' dictator, he'll sack his band every fookin' week', but the way I see it is, them musicians, y'have to watch them, always ready to get pissed . . . Cheers mate . . . and shout their mouths off about things they know nowt about. The fuckers.

ON THE SARTORIAL NICETIES

As a band, we've always dressed sharp. You have to. That Oxfam shop on Salford High Street sells some all right stuff at a fair price. There's times I've taken the whole band in there – well, them that I hadn't fired that morning – and had them kitted out with flares and red-and-white tank-tops. Nobody rates a scruff. Not that I've ever really bothered about clothes, mind . . . [continues endlessly].

MAD WORLD:
EVELYN WAUGH AND THE
SECRETS OF BRIDESHEAD
PAULA BYRNE

. . . It is really rather surprising how Evelyn Waugh's relationship with the Starborgling family of Starborgling Court, Loamshire, and its absolute centrality to his literary career, has so far escaped the attention of critics. In fact, aside from the seventeen authorised biographies, the multi-volume edition of his letters, the ten-part television series presented by Nicholas Snargs, and Lady Stultitia Blodwyn's exquisite memoir, scarcely a single book and barely a dozen or so scholarly articles have dwelt in even the most incidental way on the Starborglings' extraordinary influence on his great masterpiece *Bargshead Revisited*.

Although Waugh had known The Hon. Hyacinth 'Fruity' Starborgling (famous for remarking, on the occasion when a crowd of Mayfair debutantes were caught in a hailstorm, 'My dear, it didn't rain, it Diored') at Oxford, where they were both members of the Rectum Club, his real introduction to the family of Earl Starborgling, and in particular his daughters the Ladies Mortitia, Venetia and Drusilla, did not come until 1931. 'Darling Bonkers,' runs one of his characteristically witty effusions to Lady Venetia from around this time, 'I don't suppose you'd let me be your chum, would you? I'm afraid I didn't go to Eton like Fruity and my wretched father is horribly middle-class, but if you could see your way to overlooking this I'd be most fearfully chuffed. Please ask me for Christmas – it would be just too super. Just off to roger a tart, so let's hope the old cock doesn't drop off eh?'

In old age Lady Venetia would remember the sensation that these letters produced at the breakfast table. 'He was just so frightfully funny that we all loved him. Of course it was rather sad that he couldn't find anyone of his own class to associate with, but father always said we should be tolerant towards members of the lower orders who got above themselves, and of course he'd been very kind to Piers when they were at Oxford, carrying his bags and doing his essays and so forth, and so whenever anyone found him hiding under the sofa the day after we'd seen him off on the train, we were always terribly amused: it was almost as funny as the time father shot the gamekeeper and the blood dripped all over the antimacassar.'

Surprisingly, no previous biographer has ever remarked on Waugh's momentous encounter with

Lord Starborgling, which I am able to date to an afternoon in May 1932, when Waugh, entering the gentlemen's lavatory at the Drones Club, found his lordship, well known for his ability to handle servants, engaged with one of the attendants. 'Christ, aren't you that ghastly little parvenu who writes smutty letters to my daughters?' Lord Starborgling is supposed to have remarked. No finer example of Waugh's aristocratic beau ideal could have been imagined. It is not exaggerating to say that the scene resonates throughout Waugh's later work. Clearly when Sir Basil Digby-Vane-Cretin in *Next Stop White's* is loudly sick into the waste-paper basket, Waugh has in mind the antique vomiting basins designed by the third earl and brought out at Starborgling only on ceremonial occasions such as the annual Roasting (always spelt 'rosting') of the Tenants. Similarly the celebrated scene in *Bargshead* in which a footman is sacked for referring to 'note paper' rather than 'writing-paper' can only have its origins in . . . [*continues for several hundred pages*].

. . . In later life, although Waugh maintained a charming correspondence with his old friends – 'Darling Bonkers,' he wrote as late as 1959, 'isn't life foul? Even the Pope is a bloody liberal' – it was clear that the heady days of their first acquaintance could be no more. Lady Mortitia, who died in 1981, became an authority on port wine and sitting in chairs. Lady Venetia, alternatively, made a puzzling and short-lived late marriage to the flamboyant Sir Robin Gaye-Ladd, who is thought to have left her his collection of *duchesse brisées*. Lady Drusilla, after enjoying well-publicised affairs with the Dalai Lama, His Holiness Pope John-Paul II, Rolf Harris and many other prominent men, devoted herself to the Mastership of the local Vole-hounds, in which capacity she was an august presence on the Starborgling lawn on meet days until her 109th year . . . [*continues endlessly*].

WILD MARY: A LIFE OF MARY WESLEY

PATRICK MARNHAM

... It was at this point, with the storm-clouds gathering over Europe, that Mary took the opportunity to sever her brief alliance with the Hon. Edmond Crackwytte, Lord Clantantrum's eccentric heir, and fall wholeheartedly into the arms of Reggie Kent-Cumberland, first met on an excursion to the Bavarian alps as long ago as 1932.

'War,' she later wrote, with her customarily penetrating shrewdness, 'was a splendid excuse for people to behave even more appallingly than they would otherwise have done.' Although the affair with Reggie was of brief duration (27 May to 1 June 1940) she remained grateful to him. 'Reggie was most awfully sweet. He used to lend me his copy of the *Times* and would always stand one a lunch at the Ritz and that kind of thing.' Indeed, there is an echo of the relationship in her second novel, *Frightfully Posh*, in which Salmonetta Frink-Parsnip, bathing naked off the rocks of Pollwiddlem with Hector Fitzboodle, is shocked by the size of his genitalia. 'Of course, Reggie was hung like an orang-utan,' a friend recalled, 'only one didn't talk about such things in those days.' Now, with her children lashed to pushchairs in the care of an obliging factotum, Nanny Fang, and her husband off somewhere or other, Mary was able to join the 'top secret hush-hush Whitehall show' run by her Old Etonian friend Walter 'Carrots' Cholmondeley, and accumulate the valuable experience that was to see her, many years later, emerge as one of the most tedious upper-class drips in modern English letters [*shouldn't that be 'distinguished lady novelists'*? Ed.].

LIST OF ILLUSTRATIONS

Mary's great-great-grandmother, Henrietta ffrench-Saunders, painted in Rome by Garibaldi, RA

October 1933 En route to India with Bobo, Oofy and Gervais

July 1941 Christening of the Hon. Toby Snargs, St Philomena's, Pendennis-on-the-Tamar

FROM THE INDEX

MISCELLANEOUS TRIFLES

ALBION: THE ORIGINS OF THE ENGLISH IMAGINATION
PETER ACKROYD

i THE TREE

The poetry of England is born in a glade hedged round with the shadows of the ancient trees. Made of wood, ever sprouting their charming and tremulous leaves, their roots extending far underground, bark-adorned, they bring mystery and enchantment to the poetic imagination. Thus Sir Hugh de Hee in his fifteenth century 'A Pretty Chaunt to ye Verdant Woodland' remarks that:

> A canopy of grene fronds dost ere enclose
> The wood wherein my ladye goes

In much the same spirit, four hundred years later, the Lincolnshire dialect poet Silas Bole intriguingly observes:

> Alas! The lofted arching tree!
> That harbinger of melancholy

> Ash and elm and oak and larch
> Proud sentinels of my funeral march

Tennyson, clearly, had seen a tree, otherwise he would not have been able to write 'Come into the Garden Maud'. In *Lady Chatterley's Lover* there is a fascinating conversation between Connie and Mellows: 'What is that large tall thing in the field with bits sticking out of it?' 'Don't be so bloody soft lass, 'tis a tree.' Potent, symbolic, tall, thin, often with green decorations, the tree bestrides the interior life of England.

And yet this is no calm and sequestered bower. Trees can fall down. They can sicken and die. The Plantagent poet Eorpwald the Lame writes of a birch tree that 'fell upon this mannes head/and presentlee did kill him ded'. A fourteenth century legend records the arrival in the English forests of the giant *Ag-royd* who, together with his demonic helpers Chatto and Windus, sets out to fell the mighty oaks in order to 'render them into countless bokes fit for Master Ottaker's remainder traye . . .' [*continues for hundreds of pages*].

A PEOPLE'S HISTORY OF BRITAIN

REBECCA FRASER

FROM THE PREFACE . . .

How well I remember, as a young girl, sitting at tea in the nursery at Campden Hill Square and being read to, by our governess Miss Chasm, from that most estimable volume, Mrs Bute Prendergast's *Precious Albion: a genteel and patriotic history* (1894), a work forged in an age when our Imperial responsibilities were a source of satisfaction rather than disquiet. Needless to relate, time's winged chariot has swept on since this dauntless lady first appraised her quill. Clio, the muse of history, has gathered up her skirts and skipped away. A swimming pool, to a former generation, may seem only a sink to its less heroic successor.

And yet it seemed to me, embarking on this book with my three young daughters, Tantarella, Hexagon and Ariadne, in mind, that some easy framework were required to guide members of the general public through the shooting gallery of contending arquebuses that is the historian's disputed fact. Furthermore, it appeared to me that our debt to certain gifted individuals in our nation's past was such that it behoves us to celebrate their achievements in no very niggardly manner. Sir Winston Churchill, for example, was a great statesman who contributed in a by no means unremarkable fashion to our military dispositions at a time of considerable international strife. Others there are that go unsung, such as Mrs Stultitia Blodwyn, originator of that both elegant and necessary feminine garment, the crinoline. Yet all have their undoubted place in a rich and picturesque tapestry, vivid in its outlines, savage in its extremities, pitiless in its judgements. Doughty knights on their arm-girt steeds, noble ladies on their brocade-bridled palfreys, churl and chamberlain, serf and seneschal – all march side by side in this unforgettable panoply . . . [*continues*].

FROM CHAPTER ONE: 'ROMAN' . . .
Everywhere in this storm-tossed island, shorn of its last defenders, muscular, hairy-breeched barbarians came ravening upon the sorry British and put them to the sword. All were horribly murdered, often with considerable barbarity. A ravened upon and despairing people, these Romano-British perhaps exemplified the spirit that we associate with their more lusty descendants: quiet yet unyielding hope. But it was not to be . . . Hastings . . . Agincourt . . . 'My Kingdom for a Horse' . . . Good Queen Bess . . . Noll Cromwell . . . 'We are not amused' . . . [*continues*].

THE GOOD BOOK: A SECULAR BIBLE

A. C. GRAYLING

WISDOM

CHAPTER I

1. The wise man has no fear, either of the strong or of the weak, the just or the unjust. He fears neither repetition nor prolixity. Above all, he fears not platitude. Somewhat obvious statements about human endeavour dressed up in quasi-scriptural prose have no terrors for him.

2. Gloves make a poor present for a man with no hands.

3. One does not moisten a stamp with Niagara Falls.

4. He digs deepest who deepest digs.

5. On the whole, mumps are better than measles [*continues*].

6. The wise disdain not the sagacious parable nor the ingenious metaphor, for truly these may shed more light on the doings of humankind than many a mightier work.

7. Like the lamb which lies down with the wolf in days of prosperity and is then devoured by him in times of hunger.

8. Or the small beetle which is crushed by the slightly larger beetle, having inadvertently strayed into his path [*is this right? Ed.*].

9. The wise do not hasten into speech, nor to reply, unless the request to do so comes from the *Today* programme.

10. All things take their origin from earlier kinds. Like man, horned cattle, thundering wildebeest and lesser things that crawl upon the face of the earth. All of which is proof that nature's bounty has proper origins in all its forms.

11. This, by the way, is not an argument in favour of intelligent design, which is the resort of credulous half-wits.

12. And so the wise erect their dwellings from the foundations left by those that preceded them in the development of knowledge.

13. Like the sapient bee, which constructs its nests from the debris bequeathed it by other bees.

14. Ceaselessly recycling and refashioning the words of the wise who came before them.

15. Yet copyrighting these devisings in their forewords, just like any other author.

16. The wise are tolerant, open-minded and liberally-

inclined. Their serenity is that of the cow grazing in its summer verdure, or the ox that wallows in its shady byre.

17. Unless they are asked to comment on the idea of religious belief, in which case none of the foregoing applies.

18. And their anger is that of the cow long unmilked, or the ox prodded with a sharp stick.

19. The wise judge everyone with scales weighted in their favour, unless they are members of the Church of England, Roman Catholics, Methodists and other advocates of benighted superstition.

20. The wise would quite like to be equally contemptuous of Muslims and Hindus, but these persons generally have brown skins and thus criticism of their religious beliefs is better avoided.

21. Hope is the armour of the wise, kindness their weapon, omnipresence their unavoidable destiny, an overweening consciousness of their own rectitude the pit into which the less assured among them may unthinkingly fall.

22. Like the mighty whale, which rising from the deeps, is pinioned by the fisherman's steely harpoon.

23. The wise say, 'To burn always with a hard, gemlike flame, to maintain this ecstasy, is success in life.'

24. And to write a great many ruminative articles about the nature of happiness for the *Independent on Sunday*.

25. The wise know that the right course is whatever a man deems praiseworthy.

26. Among whatever is deemed praiseworthy by well-judging persons.

27. Such as myself.

28. But the destination of all these journeys, whether it be to Broadcasting House, literary festivals, agreeable parties hosted by the *Sunday Times* Books Section, or lunches with newspaper editors, is understanding.

29. The question to be asked at the end of each day is: 'Although one is grievously over-exposed in the public prints, what are the chances of a serialisation deal in the *Guardian*?' [*Continues for thousands of pages.*]

THE YEAR OF HENRY JAMES: THE STORY OF A NOVEL
DAVID LODGE

. . . That afternoon my wife Mary and I drove to Stratford-on-Avon, a town in Warwickshire well known for its Shakespearian associations, where I had agreed to give a talk. In our publicity-conscious age writers often find themselves urged by publishers – who are, understandably, anxious to maximise their returns on the books they produce – to appear at such events: personally I find these gatherings an excellent way of receiving 'feedback' from my readers. The evening went well, and yet it contained one ominous moment. I was enjoying a pleasant conversation with a Mrs Enid Grimshaw who, I was pleased to see, had purchased two copies of my last novel at full price, when I overheard my wife at the bar asking in her usual forceful manner, 'Is there a glass of wine for David Lodge?'

As it happened, the wine had run out. Instantly I was reminded of the fateful afternoon in which Henry James, the subject of my new novel *Awful!*

Awful!, taking tea with his friend Hugh de Selincourt Heigh, and asked by his host if he would like a rock cake, looked up to find the plate empty. Was this a dreadful harbinger of the fate that awaited me? I could not be sure. However, worse was to come. Next morning, switching on my computer, an electronic communications device which many writers find exceedingly useful, I discovered an email from my agent, Tarquin Crawler. Happily Tarquin had read and enjoyed my new book. *'Dear Professor Lodge,'* he wrote, *'I just loved'* – there followed a note to his secretary asking her to fill in the novel's title – *'and am pretty sure we can flog it to Secker for fat wads of cash.'* Gratified by these words of approbation, I assured myself that I could not doubt Tarquin's sincerity, and yet a tiny bell of warning clanged in my ear. Could he not have said 'adored' rather than 'loved'? And what did 'fat wads of cash' mean? Plump? Gargantuan? I spent a troubled night.

On the following day I attended a party at The Ivy, a well-known restaurant in London's West End frequented by persons distinguished in the media, given for the novelist and son of Kingsley Amis, Martin Amis. Here I was handed a cutting from the *Guardian* newspaper conveying the disquieting news that the Irish writer Dermot O'Hermit was also poised to publish a novel about James's last year. What was I to do? Friends counselled caution.

Ian McEwan, over the course of an agreeable sand-wich luncheon – he had pastrami, I a bacon, lettuce and tomato – helpfully reassured me that 'No one's interested in Henry James anyway, David.' These stout words convinced me. I would weather the storm, I decided . . . [*continues paranoically for hundreds of pages*].

NOT A GAMES PERSON

JULIE MYERSON

This is me. Six years old and standing in a sack in the middle of a field somewhere in England a long time ago.

A sad little girl, who is always afraid. Of the hoppy bunnies who might nibble her toes with their eager mouths if she crawls down their burrows, and the cutlery that might leap up from the dishwasher and stab her if she takes her eye from its savage snarl.

Up in the sky there is a bee – could be any bizzy, little twisty bumbly bee with a blacky-brown waistcoat – but you can tell it's going somewhere far away, to some lovely flowers near the fairy ring where the pixies are gathering. And oh I wish I was going there too.

Far away from Sports Day, and sack races, and Miss Grimsditch, who is a big fat lady with bosoms down to her knees who smiles a lot but is sad too.

Like me.

[Will this do? – J. M.]

CROWN & COUNTRY: A HISTORY OF ENGLAND THROUGH THE MONARCHY

DAVID STARKEY

FROM THE INTRODUCTION

Sometimes, even when you are a case-hardened professional, you see history differently. I had one such moment when I last visited the office of my editor, Mr Jolyon Flunky, at messrs HarperCollins. At first I was faintly shocked by the way in which Mr Flunky had chosen to display only a half-dozen copies of my numerous best-selling books on his capacious shelf. But what really struck me was the presence of a very large cheque, made out to a person not unknown to me, upon the editorial desk. It was placed there, I have little doubt, out of the conviction that only I could do justice to the tantalising project that Mr Flunky now set before me.

And its presence set me thinking. Was it possible to reawaken the interest of an audience already bored beyond distraction by my recent Channel Four television series? And would it be possible to bamboozle them further by bringing together two books from the back catalogue, putting in some stuff about the Middle Ages and passing the result off as more or less new? This book attempts to answer these questions. It uses the medium of words, which I think is the only proper means of historical explanation. And the words are conveniently placed on paper, which is the only right material for a book . . . [*continues*].

ANGLO-SAXON PLATITUDES
. . . Brave Godwin! Noble Alfred! Stout Athelstan! (*Jeremy – can you check spelling of this lot? Thanks D. S.*) Little is known of these stalwart defenders of Albion's first sceptred throne, and what remains is either passingly obscure or, to be frank, not a little tedious. Nevertheless, the chronicler of this dark and inspissated epoch ignores them at his peril.

But there are occasions when, eschewing the lapidary constructions for which I am renowned, I write in short sentences.

For effect.

A MONARCHICAL PREROGATIVE MAKES A POOR CHAPTER-TITLE!
The learned commentator frequently assumes that an historian occupies some remote and occluded promontory over which the tides of popular culture,

and indeed popular expression, have long ceased to sweep. Take it from me, baby, they're wrong about that. I can mix it with the best of them. Oh yes! Look at the South Sea Bubble, when the fat was in the fire, everyone got their fingers burned and, even worse, seemed to have them in the pie. On the other hand, some of the best chapters end with a stark, no-nonsense question. I have written 300 pages of this kind of thing thus far. Can I extend to a further 200? It is precision of this kind that separates the top-level performer from the tribe of inept, and alas untelevised, amateurs who bumble along in his wake.

SEX
Of course, Victoria and Albert were at it like rabbits, you know . . . [continues].

A LOYAL CITIZEN WRITES
. . . Prince Charles, in my humble opinion, is sadly underestimated, a leader in his chosen field, for which a good description might be 'charitable entrepreneurship', an altogether titanic figure whose succession to his thousand-year throne can surely not long be delayed and whose imaginative vision politicians would do well to emulate. If one may suggest a fresh orbit into which this new kingdom of the mind, spirit, culture and values

might profitably stray, it would be the question of knighthoods for distinguished television historians whose Herculean labours have, alas, thus only been marked by the reward of a trumpery CBE. Naturally, these remarks are wholly disinterested. I cannot stress often enough that my only desire, as in every aspect of my historical research, is to see justice done and merit given its due